Mrs. Grossman

The meager spit of land, top right, is where Shackleton's men survived four months until their rescue by "The Boss". It started to snow and we were cold.

DESIGNER SCRAPBOOKS

with

Mrs. Grossman

Sterling Publishing Co., Inc. New York
A Sterling/Chapelle Book

Chapelle, Ltd.:
Jo Packham
Sara Toliver
Cindy Stoeckl

Editor: Melissa Maynard

Art Director: Karla Haberstich

Copy Editor: Marilyn Goff

Staff: Kelly Ashkettle, Areta Bingham, Donna Chambers, Emily Frandsen, Lana Hall, Susan Jorgensen, Jennifer Luman, Barbara Milburn, Lecia Monsen, Suzy Skadburg, Kim Taylor, Linda Venditti, Desirée Wybrow

Photographers: Ryne Hazen and Steve Aja

If you have any questions or comments, please contact:
Chapelle, Ltd., Inc.,
P.O. Box 9252, Ogden, UT 84409
(801) 621-2777 • (801) 621-2788 Fax
e-mail: chapelle@chapelleltd.com
web site: www.chapelleltd.com

Library of Congress Cataloging-in-Publication Data

Grossman, Andrea.
Designer scrapbooks with Mrs. Grossman / Andrea Grossman.
p. cm.
"A Sterling/Chapelle Book."
ISBN 1-4027-1058-5
1. Photograph albums. 2. Photographs--Conservation and restoration. 3. Scrapbooks. I. Title.
TR465 .G78 2004
745.593--dc22
2003023621

10 9 8 7 6 5 4 3 2 1

Published by Sterling Publishing Co., Inc.
387 Park Avenue South, New York, NY 10016

Distributed in Canada by Sterling Publishing
c/o Canadian Manda Group, One Atlantic Avenue, Suite 105
Toronto, Ontario, Canada M6K 3E7
Distributed in Great Britain by Chrysalis Books Group PLC,
The Chrysalis Building, Bramley Road, London W10 6SP, England
Distributed in Australia by Capricorn Link (Australia) Pty. Ltd.
P. O. Box 704, Windsor, NSW 2756, Australia
Printed in China

Sterling ISBN 1-4027-1058-5

This volume is meant to stimulate craft ideas. If readers are unfamiliar or not proficient in a skill necessary to attempt a project, we urge that they refer to an instructional book specifically addressing the required technique.

Table of Contents

ADVENTURES IN

25 Years with
Mrs. Grossman's

Many people don't realize that Mrs. Grossman's Paper Company actually began in 1975 with a completely different product line. The business was housed in various odd locations and was largely run by myself and my eleven-year old son, Jason.

START

In 1979 the first sticker, a red heart, was created, launching an industry. Stickers became a new art form.

Our immediate success took us into new headquarters as well as to countries around the world.

Stickers began to come in all sizes: bears, giant bears, and baby bears.

Kids were collecting stickers like crazy and we created products to put them on and in.

In 1984, shimmery opalescent stickers were born.

In 2004, another industry first at Mrs. Grossman's—textured stickers for scrapbooking and crafts!

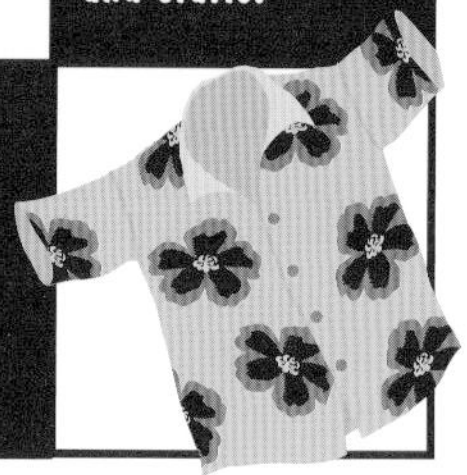

In 2004, Mrs. Grossman's began the next 25 years!

STICKERLAND

In 1990, famous mime Robert Shields brought his talent and the human figure into the line.

1991 saw the introduction of the Extravagant stickers with our lovable rabbit.

1993 premiered the new collection of "Sparkle Stickers", images printed on holographic material. The kids can never get enough of them.

In 1995, the company moved to its present site in Petaluma.

Design Lines were introduced in 1997, setting another trend in the industry.

The beautiful Photoessence line joined the family in 1998.

In 1999, the amazing laser-cut stickers, Paper Whispers, were introduced.

In 2001, not only do the Favorite Albums debut, but the expansion of the building provides the company with a store and museum.

Busy 2002 brought the wildly popular Vellum Collection, another industry first and the nature-themed Studio Line by Zeke Smith.

Industry leader Dee Gruenig teamed up with us in 2003 to produce the Posh Impressions line.

Introduction

The Beginning

As I sit at my desk, beyond my window lies a beautiful bird sanctuary, and across a lake, the golden rolling hills of Petaluma, California. All around me are the people of my company, joyfully going about their various tasks. I am filled with awe and gratitude, for I have been truly blessed in my life with my family, friends, career, and faith.

When I started out making Mrs. Grossman's stickers; my young son Jason was my first employee, in charge of shipping. I had no idea what would happen, but I trusted that my life followed a divine path—I just had to hang on and see where it would lead. Now, it has led me to the rewarding, family-centered activity of scrapbooking, which has allowed me to preserve and celebrate many of my own great family memories and, even better, help others to do the same.

I grew up in Pacific Palisades in Southern California at a time when childhood was more carefree than it is now. In that benign climate, we could run and roam and ride our bikes all over in total freedom, without fear of any kind. My mother stayed home to take care of her three children (I was the youngest), and my dad was a distinguished newspaperman. We were too engaged just living life to think about preserving memories or keepsakes. All you have to do is look at my baby album to see what I mean—it's an empty book with a stack of loose photos in no particular order, now brown with age.

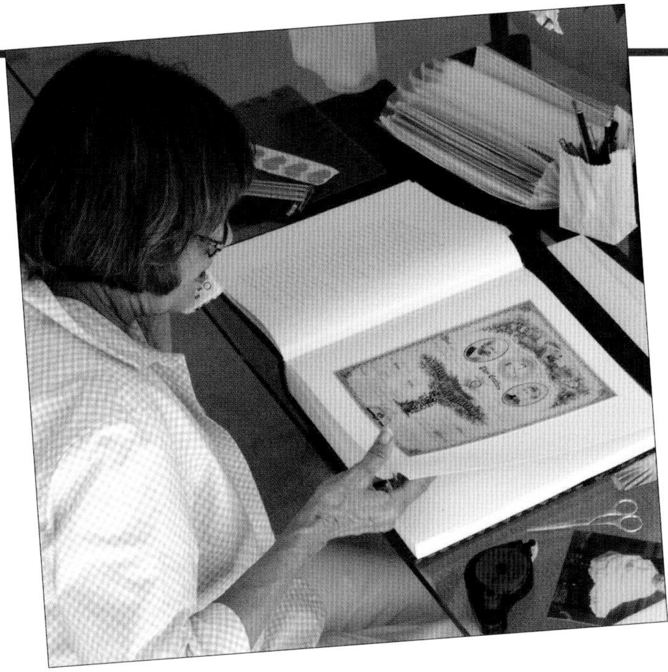

Maybe because of that, I bring a new, simple style to the craft of scrapbooking. In my books, the people take center stage. The pages are simple, drawing the eye to the main characters. I came to this style naturally, because my own design approach has always been clean and uncluttered, whether it's the offices around me, which are all soft gray and glass, my home, which is all white (despite the presence of my mostly black Australian shepherd) or my early graphic designs, which were meant to communicate rather than just decorate.

My interest in art began earlier than I can remember. My mother, a watercolorist in her own right, taught me my colors before I could even talk. One night my father brought home all the spools of thread in the Coats & Clark® line so I could touch the vivid hues that fascinated me as though they were jewels. Even today, color is vitally important to me, especially as it relates to emotion and mood. The subtle tints around me here create a calm feeling. At home, the all-white surfaces are a blank canvas waiting to be "painted on" by friends and family.

Following my natural bent, I attended the University of California, Los Angeles, to study art and then the Art Center School of Design, majoring in graphic design. I married, and after freelancing for a while, I started a small design firm in Northern California, specializing in simple motifs and beautiful papers, another longtime fascination of mine.

The Heart

From my desk today, over my right shoulder, at the edge of the Mrs. Grossman's Paper Company parking lot, I can see a white flag emblazoned with only a plain, solid red heart.

The history of it, by now, is well known. In 1979, I created the heart to be made into a sticker, and the printer sent them to me, not on flat sheets as I had expected, but 50,000 stickers on narrow rolls that practically jumped out of the box looking for adventure. My customer, Kitty of Pinestreet Papery in Sausalito near the Golden Gate Bridge, loved them, and they sold out in a flash. I did a few more simple designs and had them printed the same way—on rolls. Stickers by the Yard® was born, and it caught on like wildfire.

Today we print 15,000 miles of stickers per year, right here in this building—below where I'm sitting, in fact. Ten-color presses and a computerized laser-cutting process have enabled our stickers to be bold and vibrant or lacy and delicate and just about any shape you can imagine, from fairy dust to the Eiffel Tower. My son Jason, who has held many positions in the company, is now the vice president and manages production for the company as well as his own label company, Paragon Label.

The image on the flag means a lot more than just the first sticker that launched the company. I had prayed for work that would benefit and uplift others, as well as being fulfilling to me, and it came in such a simple, yet significant, form—the heart. The stickers that followed not only drew to me all the wonderful people who work with me, but also brought whole families together as they shared collecting and making craft projects with stickers. This fad spread all over the country and gave parents and children a new activity they could share at a time when families seemed to be drifting further apart.

New Directions

I never intended any of this. We all worked hard, but, in a way, we were lifted by the wind; and it carried me even when the bottom fell out of the sticker market. The fad fizzled almost as quickly as it had sprung up. We were left with lots of stickers and lots of bills. Once again, the Lord had revealed his plan. Talented, caring people came to my aid and carried me through the crisis.

It took time and it wasn't easy, but we came through it and were stronger than ever. These amazing "angels" who advised me and gave so generously of their time and expertise are now my board of directors.

As we got back on our feet, a lovely woman in Montana started using our stickers to enhance beautiful family photo albums she was creating with archival materials that would last for generations. The idea spread to her friends and neighbors, and through Creative Memories®, scrapbooking was born. Again, simply by the grace of God, we were part of it right from the very beginning.

This company, begun with such simple surroundings, is today one of the most electric business stories of the century.

Making a Difference

Someone asked me recently to name the happiest time of my life so far, and I said, "Oddly it was when the company was in jeopardy." True friends came forward, and all of us became a close group, supportive and nurturing of each other. I've never been one who likes things too easy. What could have been a disaster became just a turning point, forcing me to focus on priorities and define our true mission.

It became clear that I wanted to combine commerce with caring. Along the way, I have been privileged to meet some incredible people—far too many to mention all their names. One, though, was the late Julia Middleton, then the director of the Hunters Point Youth Park. Hunters Point is an economically stressed area of San Francisco. We met because I was looking for a way to share our blessings. Ms. Middleton and I developed a program together. We donate our sticker overruns and Hunters Point children, ages 9 to 13, pack them in kits that go to children in over 300 hospitals all over the world. It gives the kids some valuable work experience as well as the pride of doing something for others.

We also work with the Picture Me Foundation, which sends albums to critically ill children and parents who have lost a child so they can record their journeys as part of the healing process.

The company, which originally worked out of a child's playhouse in a San Francisco suburb, is now home to 160 employees, many of them related to one another: husbands and wives, mothers and daughters, fathers and sons, cousins, and not just a few "sweethearts." Dogs keep us all company at work. We have hundreds of guests touring our plant daily. Maybe you could be one of them soon? We would love to welcome you to the "company with a heart."

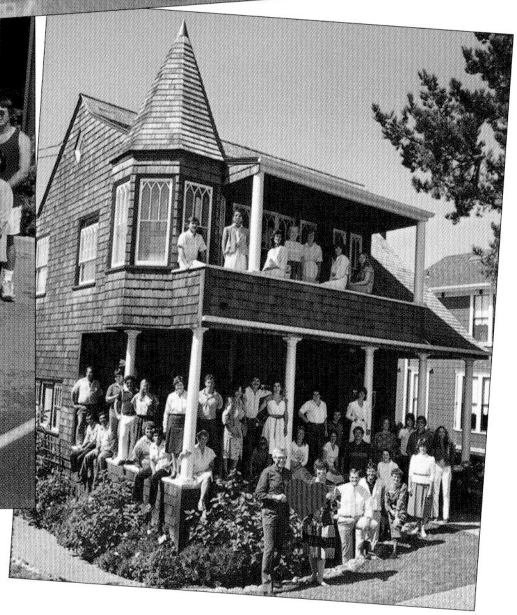

It is a privilege to be part of an industry that has such meaning and purpose. The people who are making albums are family-oriented. Parents and children are making albums together, reminding me of the early days of stickers when families worked on projects together.

Before Scrapbooking

Scrapbooking is not a part of my heritage; you can see that from my baby album. It is a craft that I have learned late in life, and I can say it has truly changed my habits of picture taking and recording events. Now, rather than throwing all my pictures in a convenient box or bag, I sort them out as I have them developed, with important events stored in individual boxes, ready for the album I plan to make.

The Art of Scrapbooking

I made my first album for my son, Jason, after we had taken a trip to the Holy Land. It was a memorable experience, and I wanted the album to include all the emotions, vistas, and history we shared. I loved the process of making it almost as much as the trip, and Jason loves his album. I experimented with different techniques to tell the story, but it was all about the photographs. To me the photographs are the stars in an album; everything else should support them and not overwhelm them.

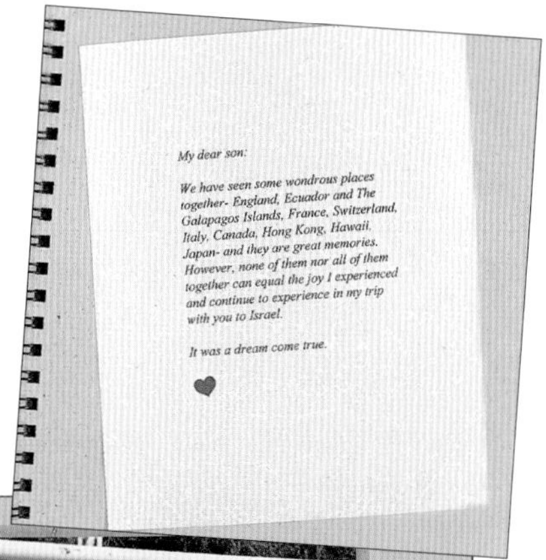

The journaling (the story) is the costar; and even if it is as simple as a word or two it is immensely important. Computer fonts are popular now, but I am a proponent of using your own handwriting. It's a little piece of you—a valuable one. In my opinion people looking at the album, especially your family, will find more meaning if it has your hand. And it will be very special for your grandchildren and great-grandchildren to have samples of your writing.

To journal, I often use a colored pen that matches the colors in my album. It looks terrific. Sometimes I even use a graphite pencil for a soft and handmade touch. You might write the journaling on a small card and tuck it in a vellum envelope on the page. I haven't done it yet, but I've seen pages that are covered with handwriting and it looks beautiful. There are phantom guides and stencils to help you keep your lines straight. I couldn't live without them.

Don't be afraid to write. In just a year you can forget details. Add names (don't forget the last name), dates, places (be specific with hotel and restaurant names—you may want to use your album for reference), ages of children, and tell the story of why you were there and what was happening.

FILM
FILM
200
We sailed on the Sea of Galilee
and walked where Jesus walked 2000 years ago.

Ready, Aim, Shoot!

I've learned to take my time when shooting a picture. Composition is so important, and worth the time to do it right. I use my zoom lens a lot, yet I don't like to rely completely on these close-ups. I like variety in scale. I try to do my cropping in the camera and I like the continuity of same-size photos on my pages—not always, of course. I often get enlargements of my better photos as a way to add drama to a page.

A few hints I've learned along the way, with some help from my dear friend, Sue Ferguson: pay attention to backgrounds—they should add to the photo or fade away; on sunny days, whenever possible, people should be in the shade; automatic cameras react to background light, so use your flash in bright sunlight to light faces; take several photos when shooting portraits or groups of people; and always choose quality film developers for excellent results.

Photography

My skills in photography have changed, too. I take time to compose the pictures rather than just snapping them. I rarely have a lamp growing out of someone's head these days, but I do have a few comical pictures of dinner guests beneath my dining-room table lights. How does that happen!

I try to focus my camera on the most meaningful part of the scene I am shooting. I watch for tangencies, making sure the background works with the subject in the foreground. For instance, in the picture of Jason sitting on the Roman aqueduct, he sat off-center of the arch, and I watched for where the horizon line connected with his body. Half water/half sky could be static, so I opted for two-thirds sky.

When I start an album, I lay out my selected photographs on the pages to see how the sequence and relationships are looking. When it is time to place the pictures on the page, I rarely measure for spacing, but I do have to stand up when I'm doing a large album so that I can get it positioned correctly. We artists call that "eyeballing."

No Paper Shortage Here!

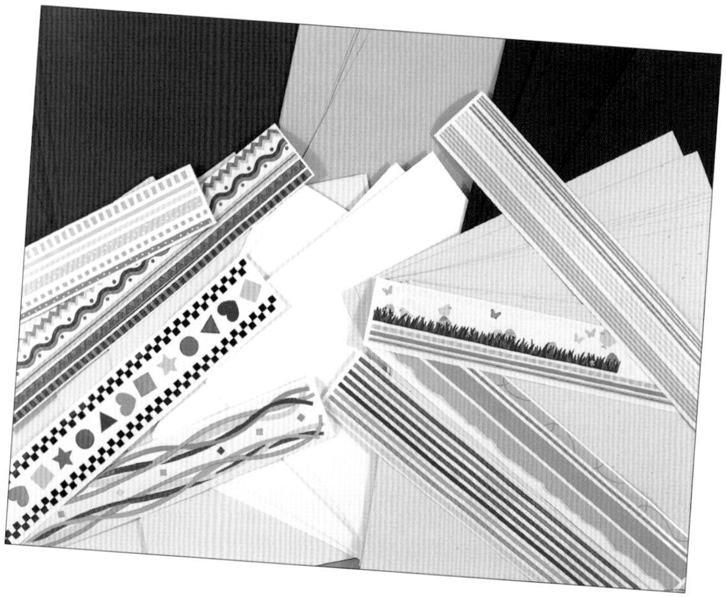

Isn't it remarkable how many papers we have to choose from? I love to wander the shelves and aisles of paper to discover just the right paper for a project I'm working on. Storing all these papers is a challenge, but I have found great storage units at a local store that I can tuck away in a closet.

I tend to use white or black papers frequently, and I love ivory. I also adore the spectrum of colors that are available, as well as the embossed papers that are wonderful to use in the right setting. I purchase multiple sheets of paper that I like and use often; because the stores are turning over their stock so frequently, it is often difficult to replace favorite papers. When a new great paper shows up, I purchase a bunch of it, even when I don't have a specific project going. I know what I like, and any paper I've chosen will find it's way into an album eventually.

Of course, I use stickers in all of my albums. I see them as "silent communicators" and use them to set the tone, make a statement or just add color to the pages. Sometimes just one sticker raised on a square panel is all I need to make that statement. Design Lines: I never leave home without them. I would be lost if I didn't have them and I use them to frame photographs, to outline journaling panels, and to finish the edges of pages. I tell stories with stickers. Stickers can make my pages beautiful, humorous, or tailored. They are simply hard workers! So easy to use—no cutting, no glue!

“Most of my albums are gifts or memories of trips and occasions.”

Packaging is Everything

Choosing an album is great fun. I keep in mind that when the album is open, the cover color will be “bordering” every page, so the color is important. There are so many good choices out there, I’m bound to find just the right one when I am embarking on a new album. I always choose a high-quality (sometimes high-priced) album; because to me there is no reason to put all that time, effort, and expense into a poor-quality album. Of course, Mrs. Grossman’s are my favorites because of their quality and the fact that the inside covers match the outside covers. The beautiful colors blend nicely with our sticker palette and complement my photographs.

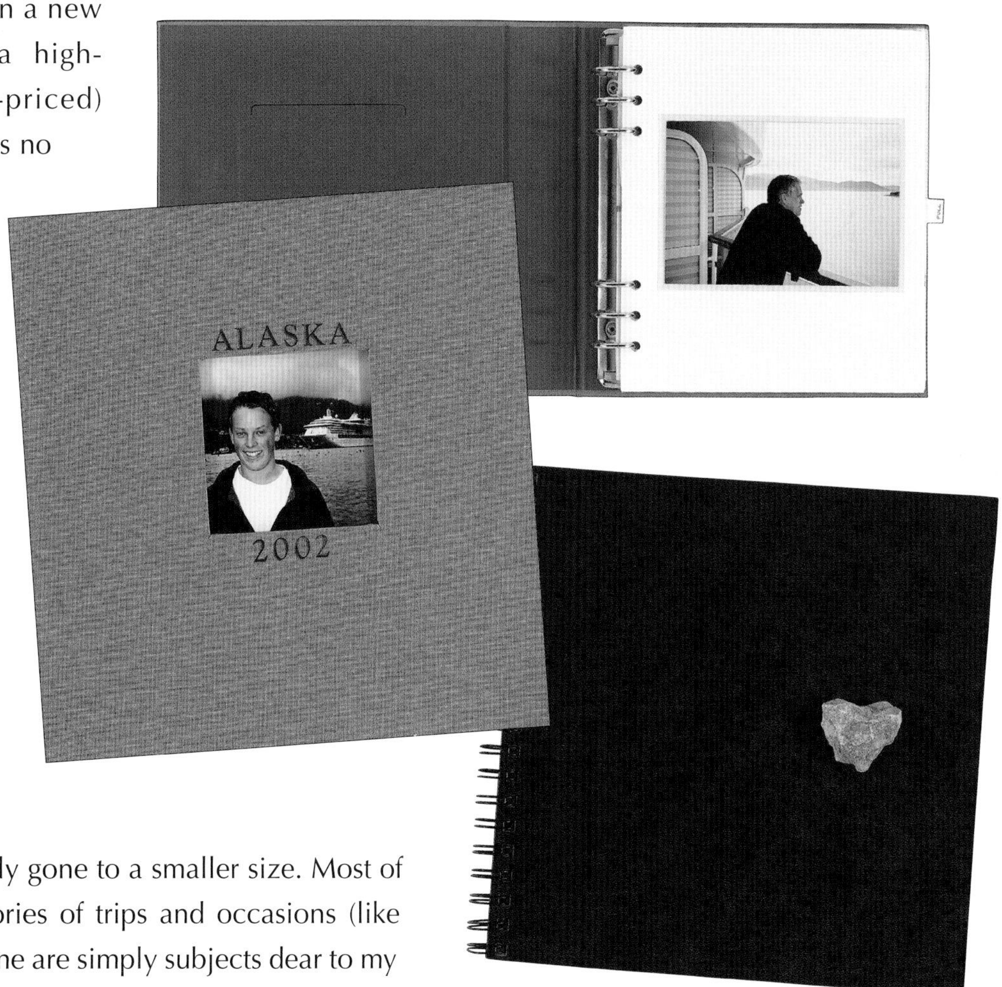

I love small albums. Jason and I have several large albums (he uses 12"-square exclusively), but I have recently gone to a smaller size. Most of my albums are gifts of memories of trips and occasions (like Jason and Kim’s wedding). Some are simply subjects dear to my heart that I like to have around to look at. I never get tired of looking through albums of my friends or of my dog Beau. They are always available on shelves or tables, and I find that other people really like to look through them.

The Mystique of Scrapbooking

It's a funny thing that when I pick up a book to read in bed, I can get through about five pages before my eyes are closed; yet when I work on my albums, I seem to be able to go most of the night. It is so inspiring to go through my photos, selecting the ones that tell the story best, then designing the perfect setting for them. Sometimes I just get nostalgic about the memories, the affection I have for my family and friends—and dog, and sit there mesmerized by the images.

Putting an album together is a work of art. For me it is an opportunity to work with paper—probably my favorite material. I've had a lifelong love of paper. Although my albums are quite simple, I like to add surprises like foldouts and flip pages to give importance to some detail. Negative space is important to me. I feel it helps to bring the eye to the focal point of the page.

At the same time, I can cover a page with a mosaic treatment (as I did in Jason's album of Israel) with photos trimmed and placed carefully together. Those pages demonstrate the noises, colors, and busy activities that we saw there.

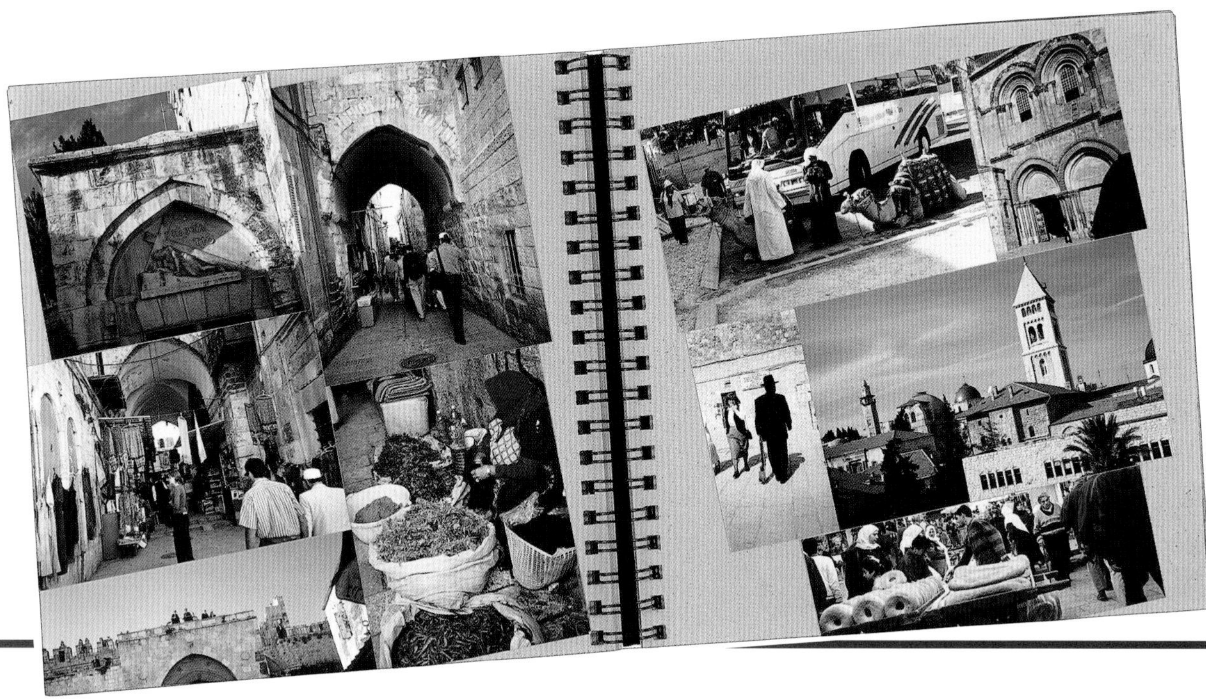

It is so easy to let the urgent take priority over the important. Scrapbooking is one way I can keep my priorities straight. My son and my friends, who will own these books someday, will know how much I love them; and I hope they will enjoy looking over them as much as I have. It occurred to me one day that I really should be putting a note in each album in my collection, designating the person I think would enjoy it most. Along with sorting out my garage, Jason will have a mighty task in figuring out just what to do with all these albums!

I encourage everyone to make a commitment to recording their family's story before it is too late. The collection of old photographs I have inherited are charming, but I have no idea who these people are or how we are related. I don't plan to make that same mistake. Recording history in the medium of scrapbooking is time consuming. But considering all the different ways we spend our time, isn't the process of collecting and highlighting the important things in your life a more valuable way to use your time?

Displaying Memories

I get the greatest gifts! I don't know if this is because I am an artist or just lucky. One of my favorite gifts, and one that I keep on my desk, is a charming sculpture commissioned by one of our sales reps from a lady in Illinois. She did 3-D sculptures of some of our stickers, with me in the middle holding our bear with a heart. If you look closely, you will see 24 sticker images. And to top it off, she made the adorable bear in his birthday hat, again holding our heart.

I do get many heart gifts. One is a dish of pewter hearts in a pretty bowl, given to me by my daughter-in-law Kim.

Another favorite gift is the giant bear who sits on the throne in my office. He was a Christmas gift from the company, and for years he sat in the passenger seat of my Datsun Z as we drove back and forth to work. Now he stays in the office and is decorated from time to time with appropriate attire. His throne is a remarkable corrugated chair, hand-painted and jewel-bedecked, presented to me at a sales meeting a few years back. The reps signed the back of the chair, and while it is a little over-the-top, I love it for the affection and memories it gives me.

We celebrate birthdays at Mrs. Grossman's! In 2003, I received maybe the most outrageous birthday card ever made. Barb Wendel, one of our artists made a paper doll fold-up card, and each member of the art department dressed the card, using only stickers, either with a look into their inner selves or a representation of the outer self. They signed the back of each figure. Of course, they asked me to identify each one before I read the back, and I did pretty well! No birthday gift could top this wonderful card, so, in order to preserve this work of art, I had a lucite display box made for it.

I love toys. When my friend Kitty Okamura gave me this wooden Indian circus, I had to display it in my office at home. As well as unique gifts, I receive so many beautiful cards. I keep some of my mementos from friends in the same shelves in my home office, protected from dust and sunlight. I keep interesting graphics from events I have attended—tickets, posters, photos. The two larger photos in the back of the shelf are from my trip to Israel and Petra with my son Jason. The straw hat is from our visit to Venice, and the cute wood sculpture is one Jason made for me when he was a little boy. I just loved the design. I also collect unusual pencils and pens and display them in hand-blown works from a local glass blower.

Basically I am not a collector; but I can't resist hearts. Whenever I travel, I bring back a heart-shaped rock from the trip. It always surprises me how many heart-shaped objects you can find—wood, glass, stone, metal. I have bowls and containers of heart-shaped objects all around the house. And of course, I am often the recipient of a gorgeous heart gift.

I live on a lagoon in Northern California. Water is where I go to unwind or to feel appreciation for all I have been given. I own a small electric boat, complete with a surrey top, where I often host dinners and picnics as we putter around the lagoon. Business meetings on the boat are far more successful than those around a table.

The wall of family photos in my home is a place where I often stand and just consider the impact my dear family has had on me. Some of the photos are in their original old frames, some I have reframed to fit the look of the wall. My father is that cute little guy in the dress!

Friends & Family .....

friends

Jason's Family Album

I have had good intentions about making an album for my son Jason. When he and his wife Kim gave me this beautiful album for Christmas two years ago, I lost my last excuse.

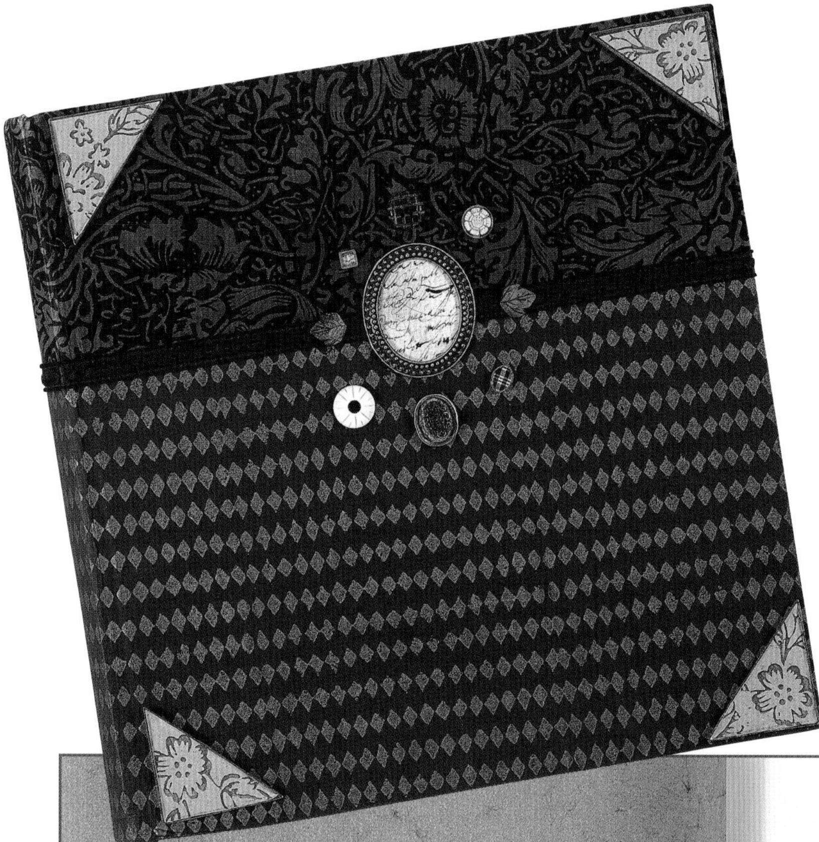

After sorting through the photographs I inherited from my family and thinking about this weighty subject for a long time, I decided on my approach. I would start with his grandparents and tell him all the things he would like to know about my parents—their vital statistics and the stories of their lives.

Jason loves history, so it was essential to tell him all these facts, the important ones and the funny ones, and what kind of people they were. Because my mother was forty when she had me, Jason never knew my father or his great-grandparents.

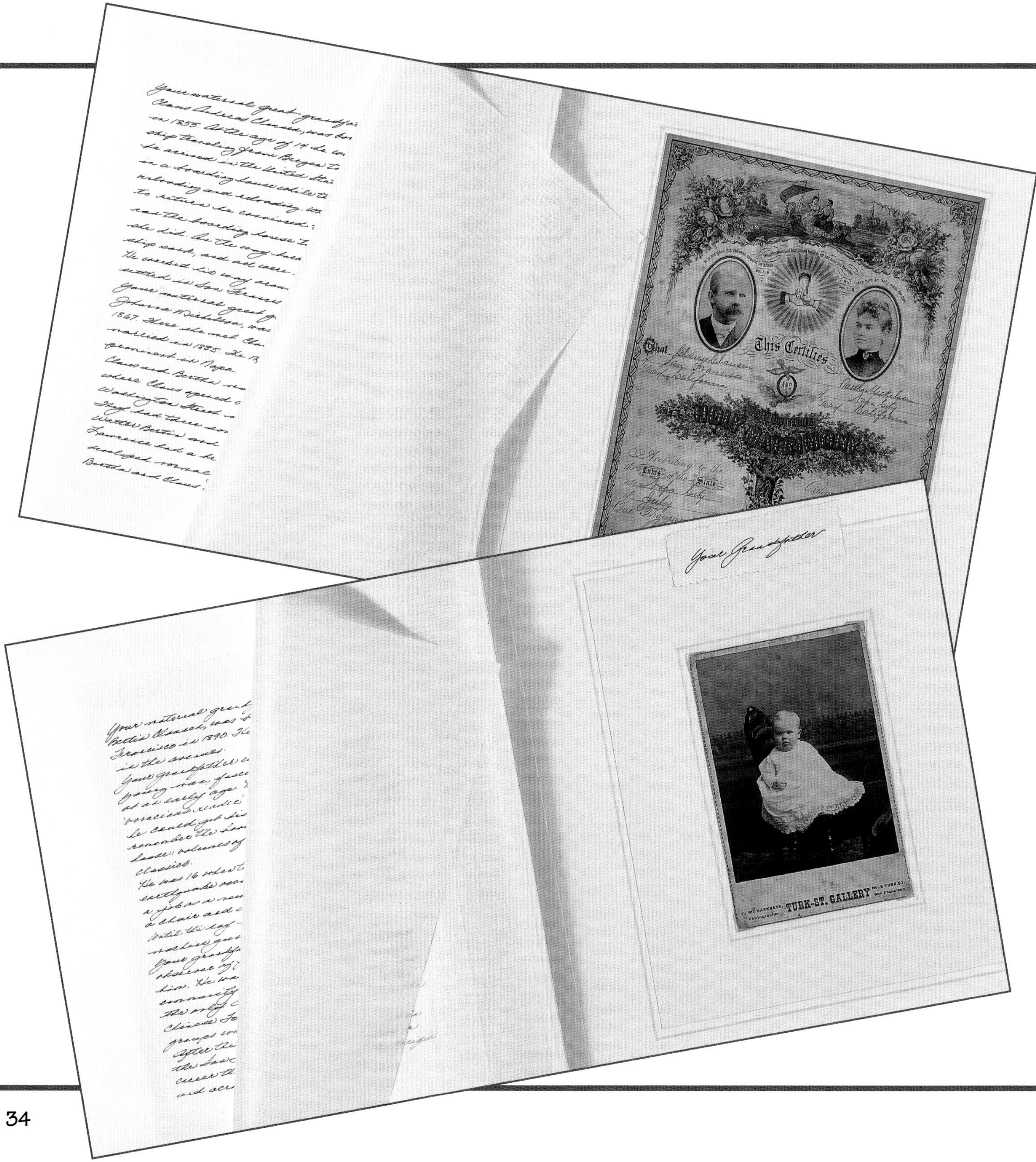
This Certifies
Holy Matrimony
Your Grandfather
TURK-ST. GALLERY

I will do the same thing for his paternal grandparents and his paternal family, probably asking his father to write the journaling about his family. Because this album is so important and so emotional, I thought it needed to be written in his own hand. I used a minimum of decoration just to add drama to the precious subjects on each page.

- It is challenging working on this book for two reasons: it is huge, and the pages are bound in with interleaves. I am mounting the photographs and journaling on paper that is applied to the pages.

Jason's Wedding Album

Together with their families
Kimberly Milicent Klain
and
Jason Hamilton Grossman
request the honor of your presence
at their marriage
on Saturday, the twenty-fourth of June
Two Thousand
at six o'clock in the evening
Viansa Winery
Sonoma, California
Reception following

Jason and Kim were married in June 2000. Even though Kim made a beautiful album for me with some of the pictures from the professional photographer, I just had to make an album of my own with some of my favorite candid shots. My girlfriends and I arranged all the flowers for the reception, which is a tradition among us. As our children get married, we gather our tools and aprons and have several days of flower fellowship. It's one of our favorite activities, and our only regret is that we are running out of marriage-age children.

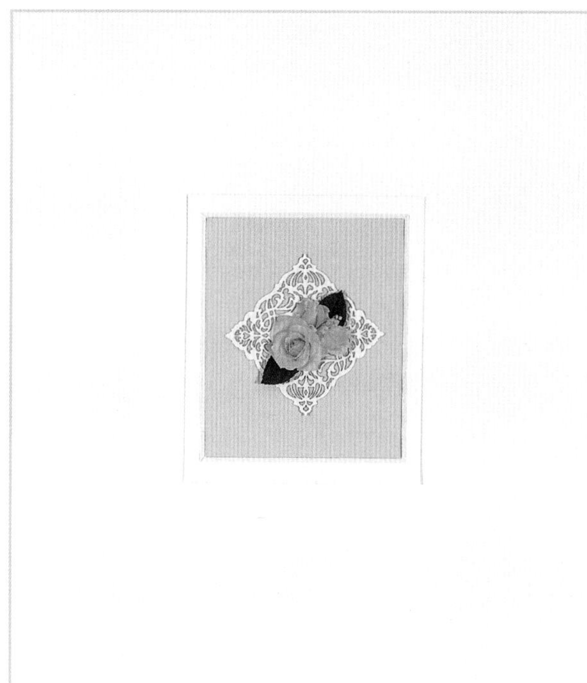

Table One
Andrea Grossman

I love you, Kim
From this day on I promise to do my utmost to make this
marriage and our new life together as passionate, loving,
exciting, and joyful as ever. I will try to make the difficult
times short and enjoyable times plentiful and memorable.
I will honor you, respect you, and care for you to the best
of my ability, using every resource that is in my grasp.
I will be patient and understanding of you as I am sure
you will need to be of me. I will always be faithful to
you in both spirit and in flesh, and in turn I will trust
and believe in you. Because of my unquestionable love
to you, I give my most valuable asset, my word, to
promise to you that I will stand by your side every
moment that is ahead of us and share a most wonderful
life with you, my wife. With God's help and with my
unfaltering devotion to you, these things I mention
will ring true from now until eternity.

• I chose our silver album, and because I knew the album wouldn't be handled too much, I cut, punched, and scored my favorite white ribbed paper to fit the album. This was a pretty simple operation: I took the paper to a scrapbook store to be cut, then made a guide to punch the holes in the correct position. I scored the paper with my bone folder and a metal straightedge.

• My friend Linda Risbrudt, with whom I often scrapbook, helped on this album. She cut the mats from the same white of the paper and the pictures were mounted on them. We have the same style of scrapbooking, so we had a real team effort creating this album. On the back cover, I attached a special note to Jason and Kim.

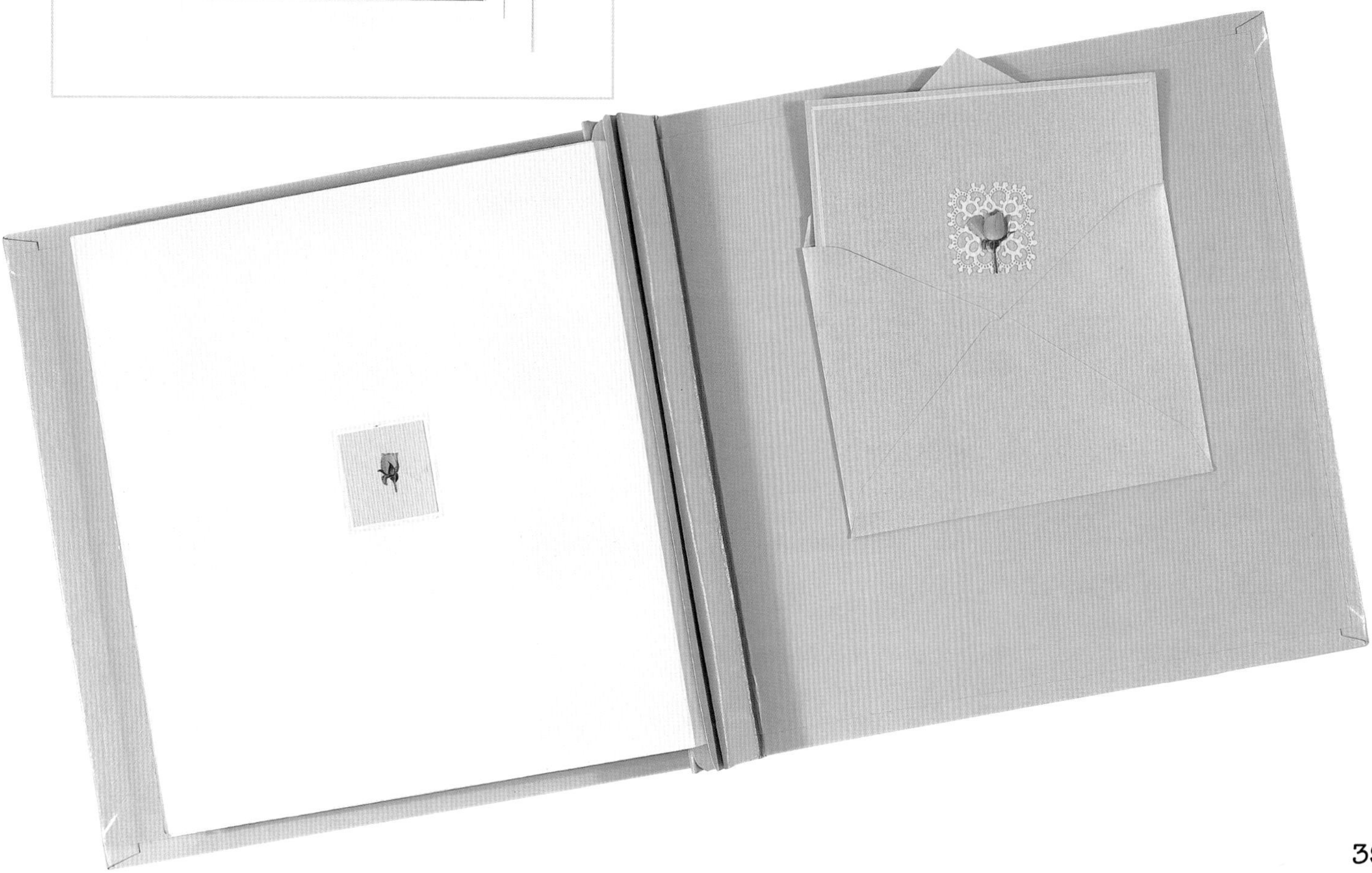

Fourth of July Albums

I love the 4th of July. I love my country and have studied its religious history and government for years. So this is a holiday that bears celebrating with an annual party at my home, primarily for family and close friends. Because I live on a lagoon, the first event of the day is a charming boat parade accompanied by cheers and whistles. After the parade we play some games focused on our history and have lunch.

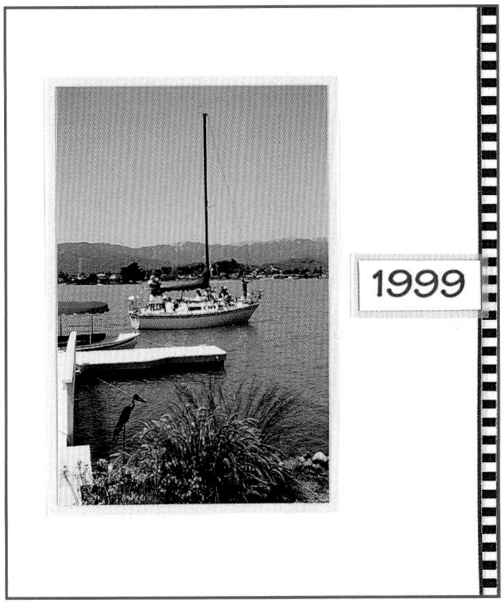

The highlight for the children is the treasure hunt, which has a theme that gives the kids a feeling for what it took to build this country, the giants in our history, and the heroism of our people. My early years are a bit skimpy on photographs; but as the years went by, we took more photos and I realized that we had a pictorial record of our kids growing up.

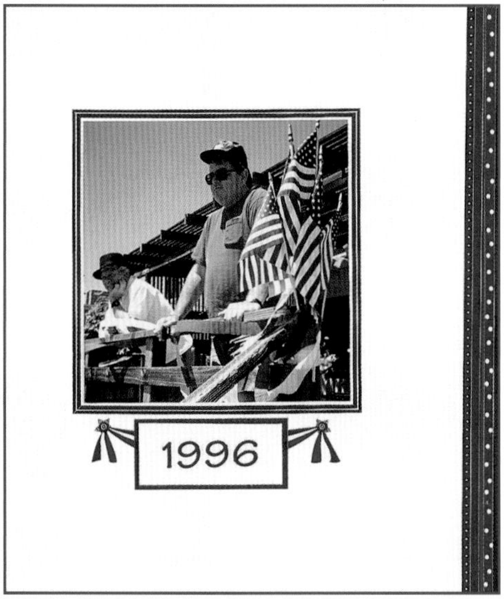

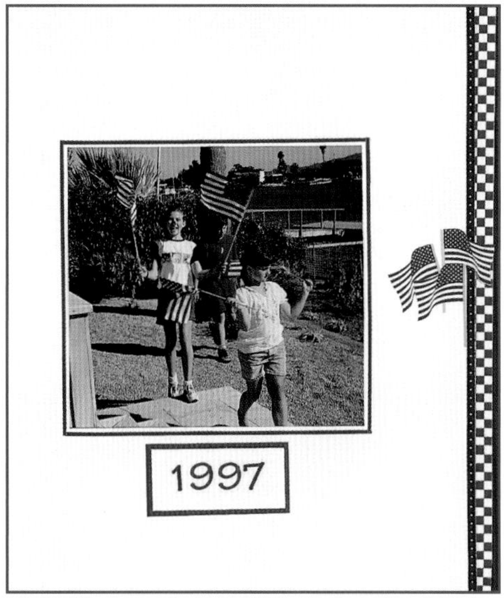

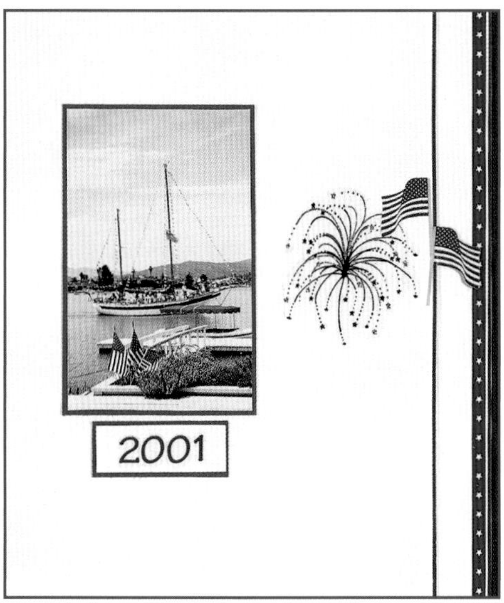

Fourth of July Albums: Volume 1

• This was the first year of the parties; and since I didn't have an appropriate photo, I created my title page by making a sticker picture of water activities.

• In order to accommodate these panoramic photos, I made a fold-out page by attaching one to the other with white artist's tape and covering the adhesive with Design Lines on the opposite side.

• To document the treasure hunt, I cut a page in half vertically and made a vellum pocket trimmed with vellum torn-edge Design Lines for the clues. I tucked in a small card describing a highlight of the game. I used the back for a cropped photo of a centerpiece.

Fourth of July Albums: Volume 2

• I used red-checkered paper to match the tablecloth. The journaling panel uses themed stickers and lots of paper layers to tell the story of the day.

• Because of my love for flag-themed clothing, I received a gift of flag sneakers, so all I needed was a red-ribbon-bedecked straw hat to complete my outfit. This is the photo I had reduced for the front cover.

• Angus is my "grand-dog," the mascot of my company, and the apple of my eye—oh, I just love this boy! There he was, wearing the crazy red hat my brother acquired in Alaska—it was the perfect touch for the day—with his white chest and incredible blue eyes! So I added red and gold Design Lines "slivers" and our wonderful fireworks stickers.

• Another treasure-hunt panel. New stickers but the same idea: I put the clues in a vellum pocket and describe the event on the back side. When you repeat certain techniques throughout a book, it saves your need to create new ideas and you can move along more quickly. In 2000, I used stickers to decorate the clue cards.

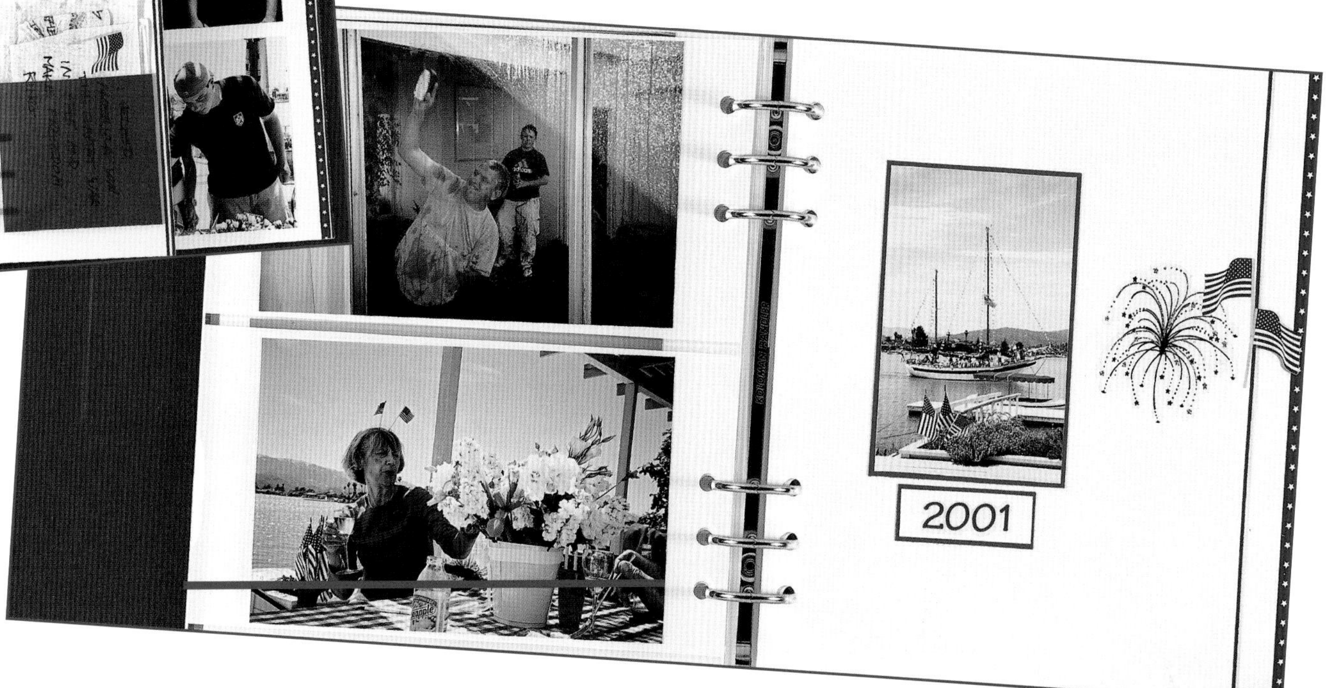

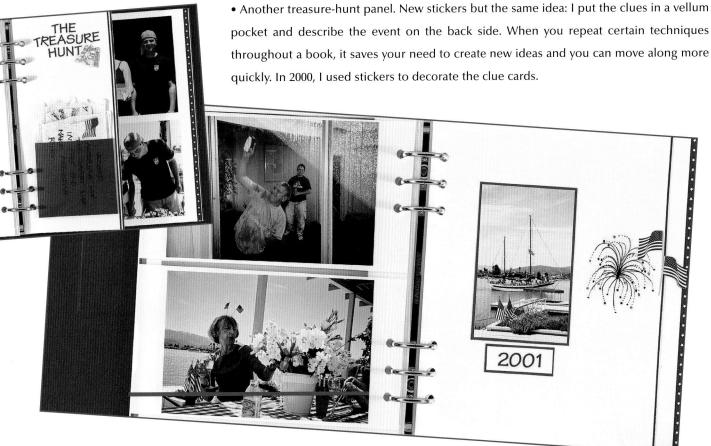

• The title page for 2001 shows an entry in the boat parade. Note each title page has a similar theme yet shows a different aspect of the event. By cropping and setting the photo off-center, I was able to emphasize the sailboat and still add a firework sticker. Again, I trimmed the page to reveal the one behind and used the flags, back-to-back, to create a page-turning tag.

• I cut a square of blue paper and added a firework sticker. After all, fireworks always end the day. I try to end a book with some symbol that says "The End."

My Friends Album

I've been thinking for years about creating a book of my friends. Lots of ideas have come across the screen. However, when I got the idea to make this book, I liked it. It's a bit corny to think of your "garden" of friends. But on the other hand, friends and gardens are two of my favorite things. Each one of my friends is a blessing to me. I love opening this book and thinking about how much they mean to me and the fun that we have had together. This is just the beginning, volume one, and I can't wait to get every friend "planted" in my albums.

• I cut and punched an ivory textured paper for this album. One special store in which I find great scrapbooking supplies has a cutter that cuts 20 sheets at a time, and a two-hole punch that punches that stack of paper.

• To make the graduated bouquet pages, I started with the last page first, trimming the edge with two shades of green vellum Design Lines. I then measured the width of those and cut the next-to-last page to that measurement. I continued in this way until I had pages trimmed from the back to the front of the album.

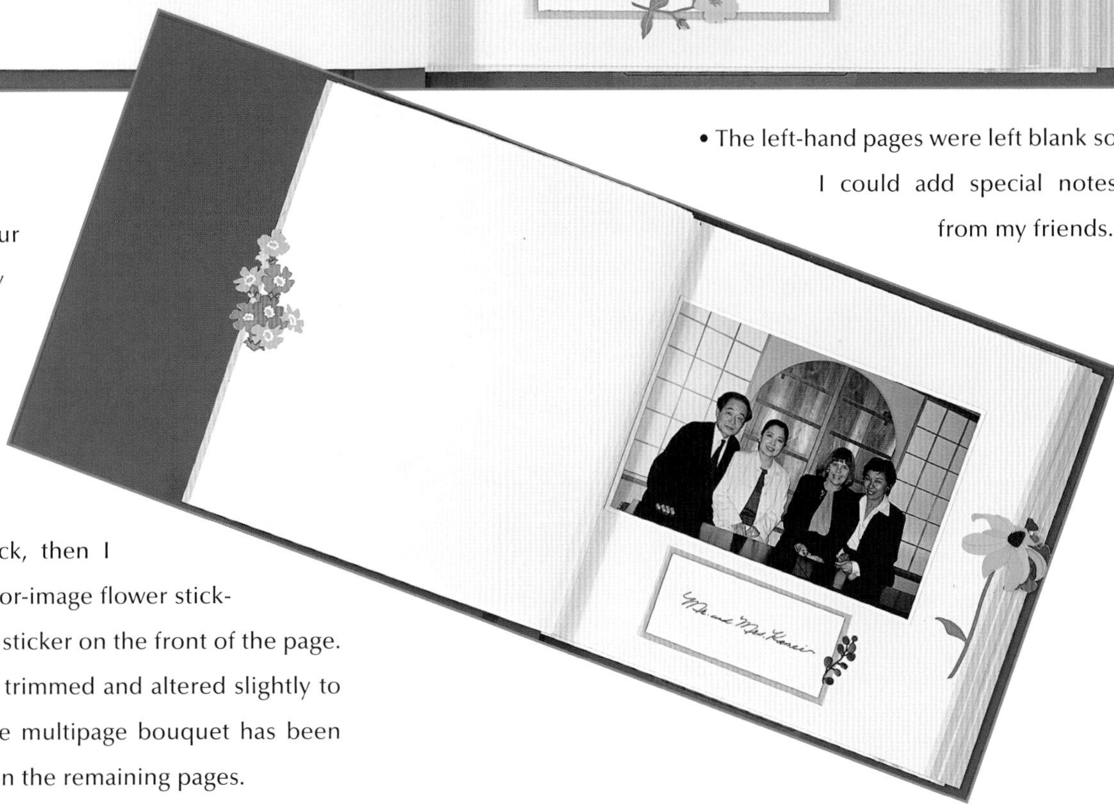

• The left-hand pages were left blank so I could add special notes from my friends.

• The flowers are from our collection and I carefully "arranged" them on the page edges over the vellum borders. On each page I put one green vellum Design Line on the back, then I carefully placed the mirror-image flower sticker back-to-back with the sticker on the front of the page. Some flowers had to be trimmed and altered slightly to fit the format. Once one multipage bouquet has been created, begin another on the remaining pages.

Friendship Cards

I like to keep a stock of cards on hand. The Friends Album inspired me to make cards using flower stickers. They are very simple and use the same technique, a panel with the flower applied to the card and Design Line sticker borders.

• To make the panel, I cut out a piece of card stock and attached it to the front of the card with foam tape. This technique allows the panel to "pop" off of the card. Then I decorated the panel with Design Lines and a flower sticker.

Tahoe Thank-you Album

• I folded a large sheet of card stock in half, then begin from the fold to make accordion folds, one for each page you plan to have in the book. Add your pages and hold the whole thing together with colorful rubber bands.

• Left: Strips of white and turquoise paper, glued together to form a slip-on band, became the method by which I held the book closed, and the medallion delivers the message of "thanks."

After spending a weekend with my dear friends Bud and Barbara at their home at Lake Tahoe, I wanted to create a small album to say "thanks" and record a few of the special moments of the weekend. This little handmade album was the result.

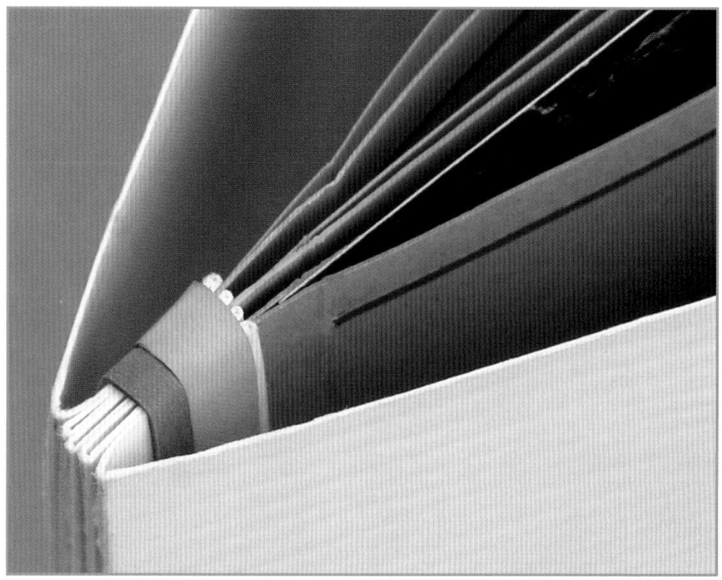

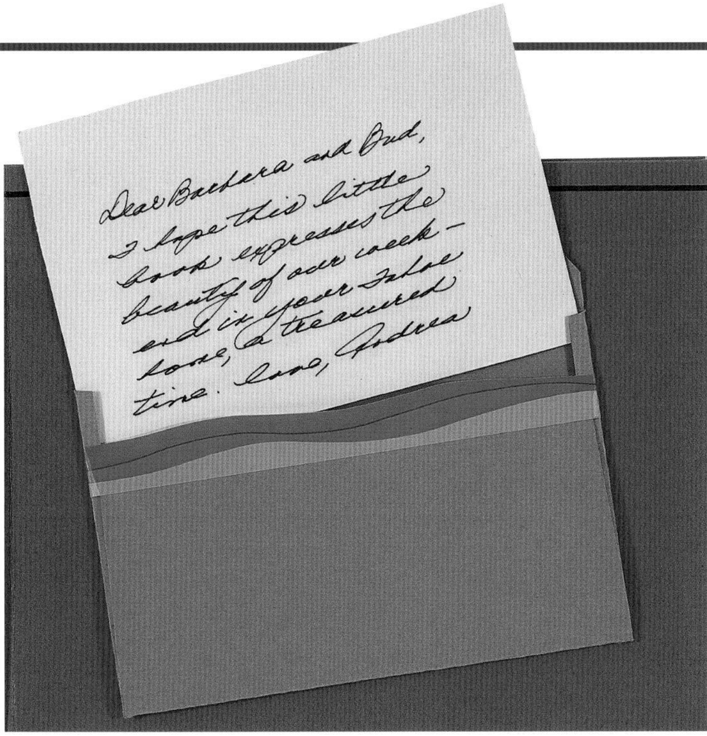

Dear Barbara and Bud,
I hope this little
book expresses the
beauty of our week-
end in your Tahoe
home, a treasured
time. Love, Andrea

• Left: An envelope on the front page, trimmed with water design stickers, holds my thank-you note to our hosts.

• I chose these beautiful shades of blue for my pages to reflect the colors of this lovely mountain lake. I thought it would be fun to have each page a different color.

• I folded the card stock in half lengthwise to create pockets to hold extra photos. A few simple sliver stickers finished off the album pages.

Virginia City Guest Album

My son and daughter-in-law have a home in the marvelous restored old Comstock mining community of Virginia City, Nevada. This town is like a living museum, with many of the citizens in authentic western gear. In fact, there are reenactments of old-fashioned gun fights in the streets every day.

This is vast high-desert country in the Eastern Sierra, and the views from the house go for miles! Kim and Jason love to entertain there and are very generous about allowing friends to use the house. It is one of my favorite places to relax, too. It occurred to me when we were there for Thanksgiving that it would be fun for them to have a guest book, so that everyone who visits could record their memories. I also incorporated sightseeing ideas for tourists to the area.

WELCOME TO THE COMSTOCK
We hope you enjoy this historic area and our home, which is your home this week. There are treasures to discover in the Comstock, and you won't even begin to discover them all in one week. Pack in as much as you can, and, if you have time, leave us a note about your adventures.
Enjoy!
Jason & Kim

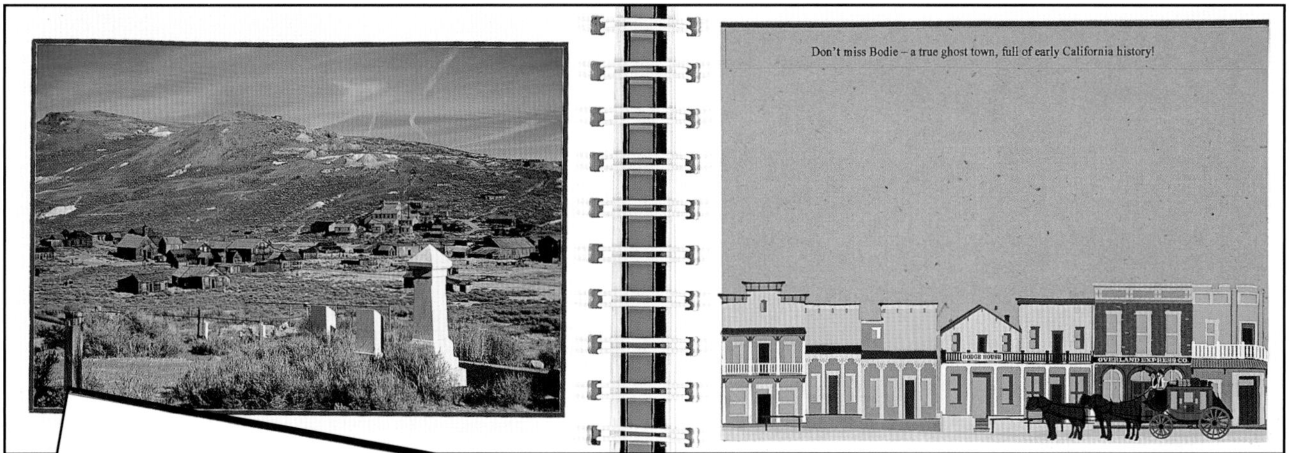

Don't miss Bodie – a true ghost town, full of early California history!
DODGE HOUSE
OVERLAND EXPRESS CO.

Or you can take a ride on the historic Virginia and Truckee railroad

• I cut panels from the same yellow textured paper that I used for the front panel and mounted them on the right-hand pages. The text is printed from the computer onto the paper before cutting. I also decided to play up the cowboy theme with western-styled stickers and Design Lines.

Baby Gift Albums

When a friend is expecting a baby, you have a wonderful opportunity to make a gift album. This can be a shower gift or a baby gift. If you know the sex of the baby-to-be, start your album well ahead of the event. You prepare the album with borders, mats, medallions, and journaling blocks. Then all Mom will have to do is add all those precious photos—no work during those busy days and sleepless nights.

Use this page for
Elizabeth Anne's
baby announcement

Baby Girl Album

• Top: For the title page, I applied a laser-cut baby buggy sticker to a piece of soft pink vellum paper, trimmed it around the edges and added a tiny pink ribbon bow. Since the sticker edges are so delicate, I chose to use an album with protective plastic sleeves.

• Left: The new mom can use the second page for the baby's name and birth date. The medallion is a vellum medallion on a square of white card stock, with vellum grass Design Line, a lamb sticker, and a butterfly sticker. The lamb is "popped" with mounting tape so it appears to be jumping through the grass.

April 4, 2002
Even though my name is
really Elizabeth Anne,
Mommy likes to
call me
her
Sweet Little Lamb

• The pages in this album are graduated in two directions from the center spread. As with other graduated pages, they were created by beginning on the last page and moving to the center. Once you reach the center, work from the first page back to the center. Here, I used ivory and pink stickers to continue the soft look of this album. The borders are a combination of vellum ribbon stickers, vellum pink ribbon stickers, vellum textile prints, vellum active edges, scalloped lace border, and lace edging Design Lines.

• Left: Vellum panels and vellum squares were used to create medallions for mounting baby chicks and lambs.

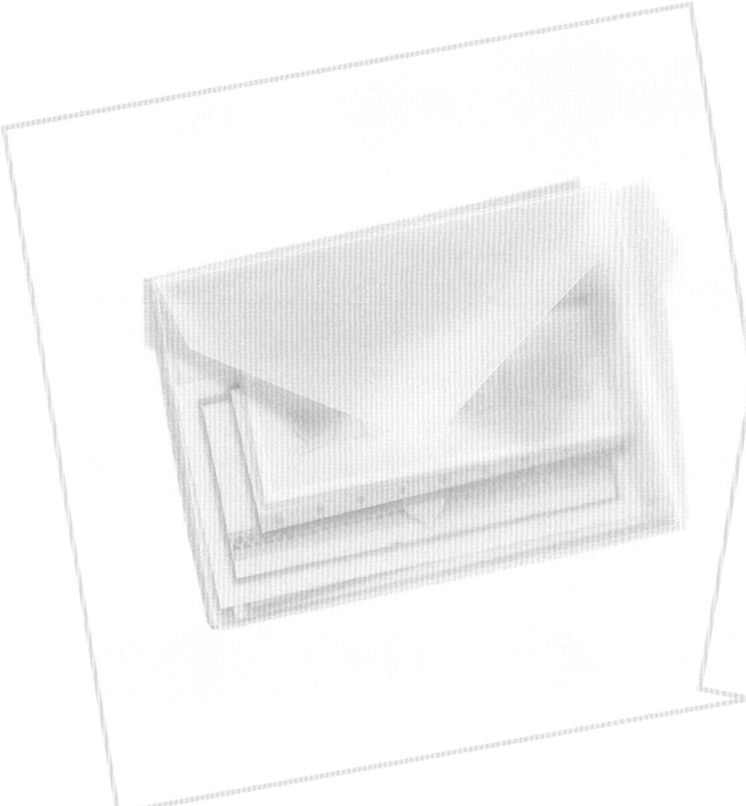

• This pink vellum envelope contains a few journaling panels that the new mother can use throughout the book as necessary, or use to complete the album with additional photos. The panels were made with the same stickers used in the book, to continue the theme. After the panels are removed, the envelope can be used for the first lock of baby's hair.

Baby Face Card

• To complete the gift, I often add a little photo mat that I decorate with stickers. A photo of the newborn is attached to the center and the mat can be placed into a ready-made picture frame. Or, the mat could be added to a page in the album.

Baby Boy Album

- Left: Design Lines on both left and right edges are back-to-back vertically.
- Bottom left: Light blue polka-dot paper is a frame rather than a mat, to make the most of purchased paper. Bottom polka-dot edging was created with cut paper.
- Bottom right: This is an example of an interacting middle page with a double window in the lower right-hand corner. To create, cut 1/8" off vertical edge; this allows for the page to interact with left/right page spreads. Punch squares, edge with Design Lines, and apply a sticker partially over the square cutout. Align the mirror image of the sticker on the back side of the paper.

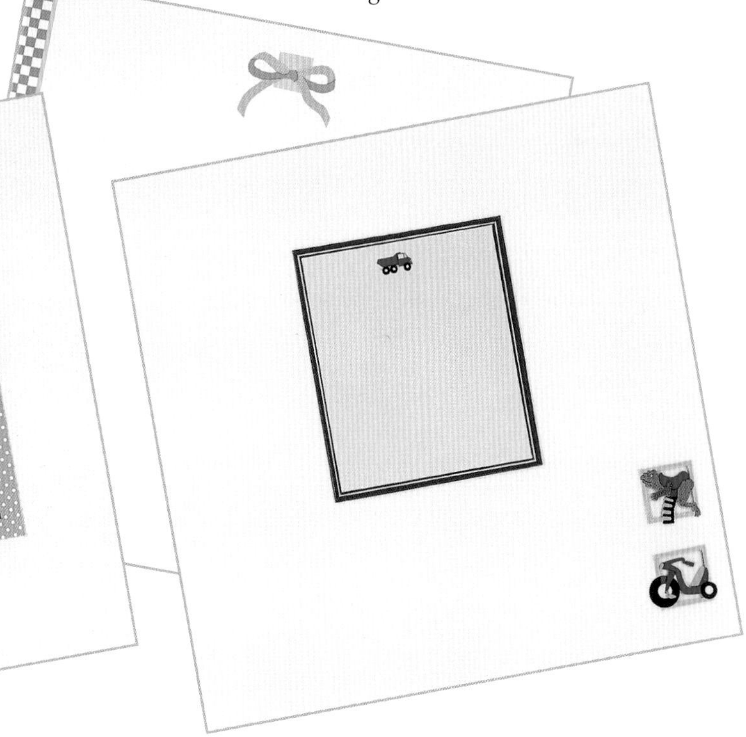

• Top left and bottom: I used color blocks to create color interest on the journaling panels.

• Middle left: Here is an example of folded journaling panel. To create, fold paper to overlap by 3/8".

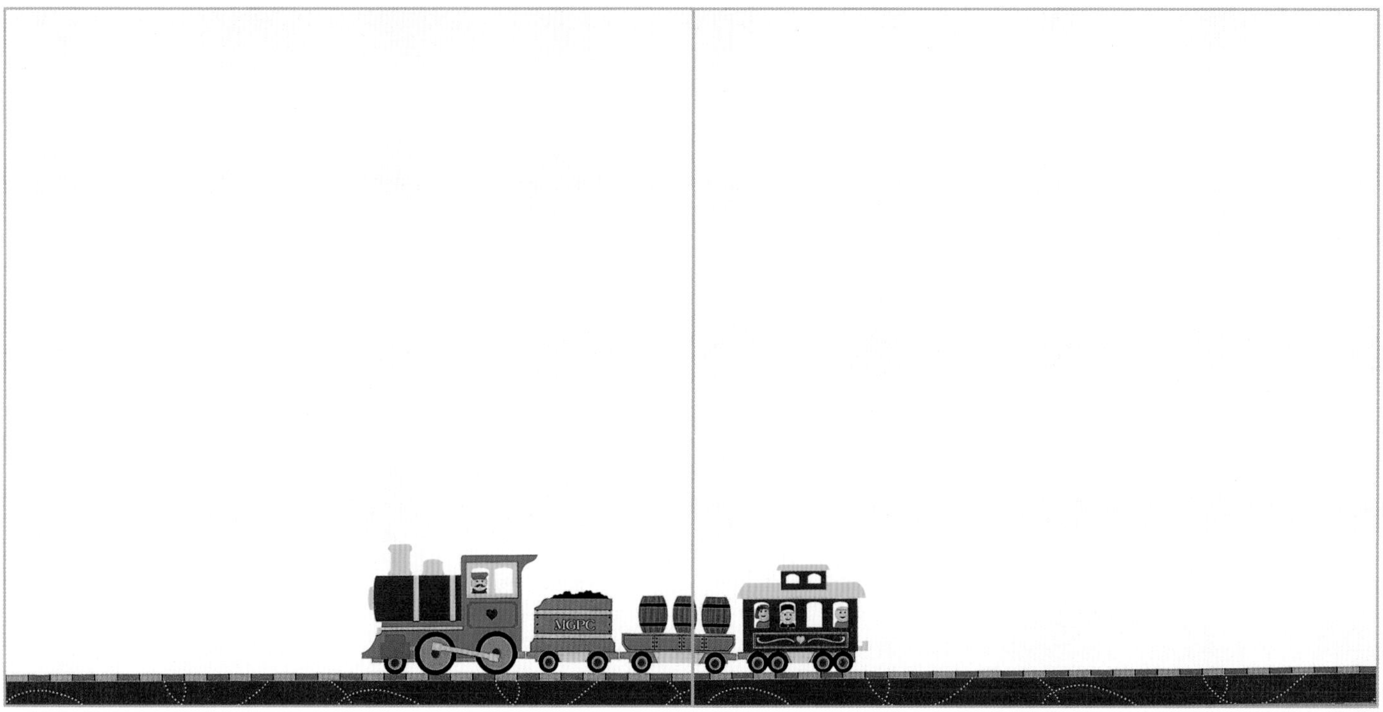

• Place pockets on both sides of one page. Add journaling cards to slide in, and use decorative scissors and a sticker to dress up the top edge. Cut a square window, using scissors or a punch. Create two square medallions to match. For a peek-a-boo window, pop one sticker on top of an identical sticker for added dimension.

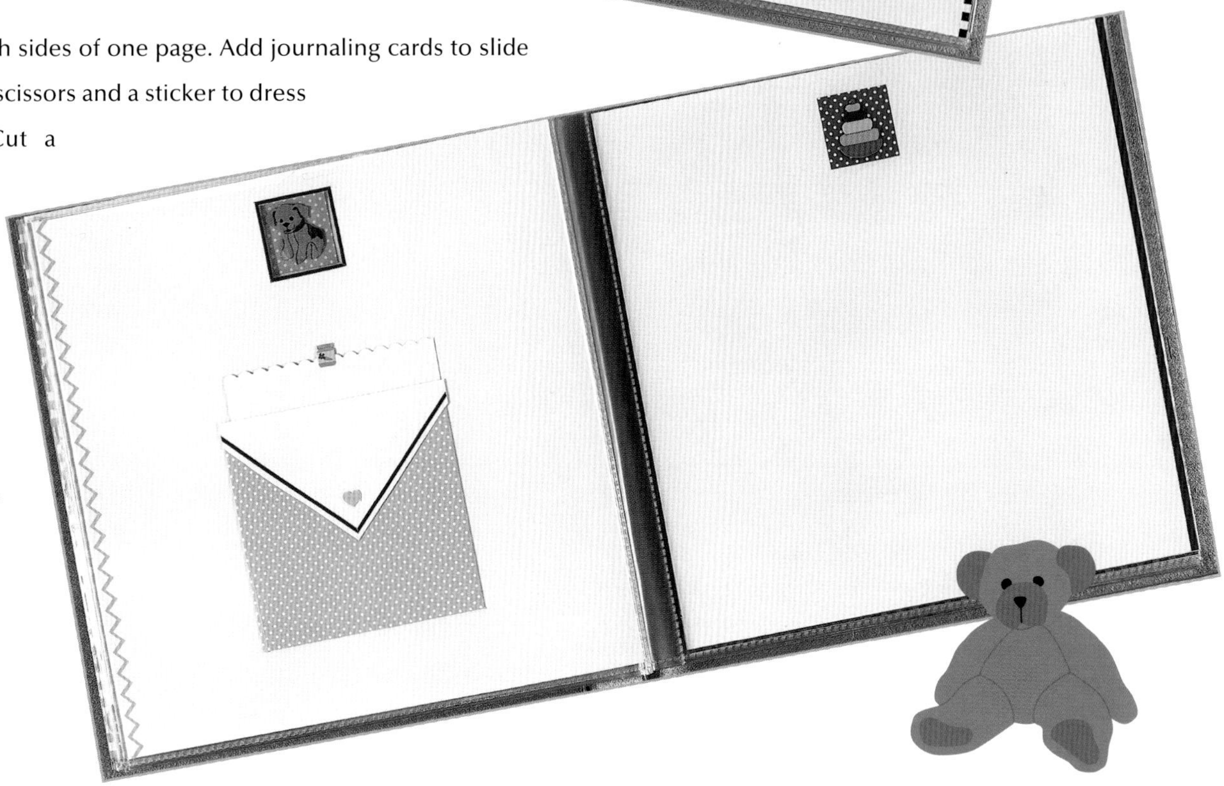

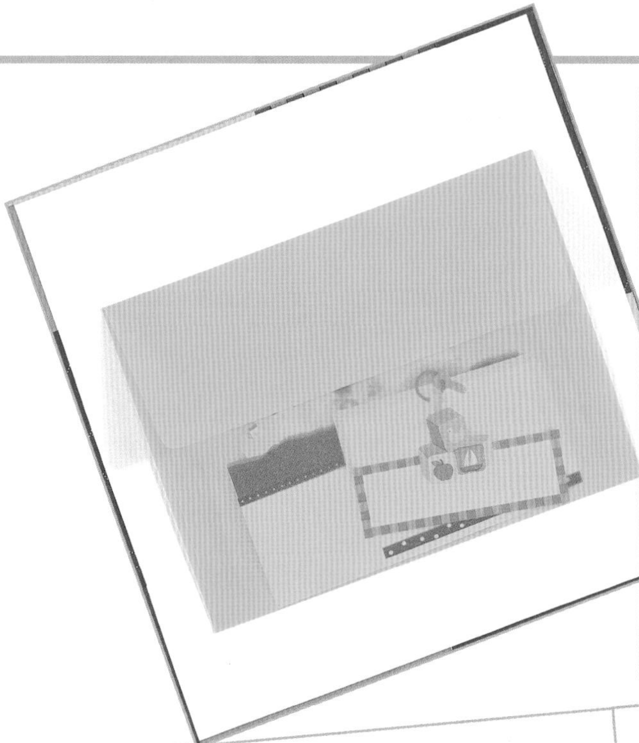

• Layer stickers behind vellum grass and arrange stickers in fun and active placements. Such an idea is to "crop-and-pop" a sticker. For example, I have cut a penguin sticker to look like it is diving in the pool.

• Use a square panel as your design guide. Write your message with the primary vellum alphabet stickers and mount a message panel over the stickers for a cropping effect.

Bridal Shower Recipe Album

When I'm planning a bridal shower, one of my favorite gifts is a recipe book for the bride. I ask each guest to bring her favorite simple recipe to share with the bride. Then at the shower, I photograph each guest. After the pictures are developed, I put the recipe book together, with a page for each recipe and author. Sometimes I send a card and ask them to handwrite the recipe; sometimes I just ask for the recipes and print them on my computer. The method depends on how I plan to design the final book.

• For this book, I chose a spiral-bound red photo journal and decorated it "sideways" so that the book could stand up on the counter. After I planned the recipe book, I gave the project to one of our artists, Kelly Corolla, and she did all the sticker art you see here. The borders are all done with vellum Design Lines, and the stickers were chosen to complement the recipes. She used mounting tape to pop some of the images. When the book was completed, we slipped page protectors on each page. This book would be a treasure for any bride.

Vegetable chowder

1/3 cup carrots, diced
2 cups potato, diced
1/4 onion, sliced
1/4 cup celery, sliced
2 tablespoons butter
2 tablespoons olive oil
1/2 cup peas
1 1/2 quarts chicken stock
1 teaspoon sugar
2 teaspoons salt
3 teaspoons chopped parsely
1 cup heavy cream

Saute onions and celery in the butter and olive oil until soft. Add potatoes, carrots, chicken stock, sugar and salt. Cover for 10 minutes. Add peas and cream. Before serving add chopped parsely.

Oatmeal Lace Cookies

1/2 cup melted butter
2 1/2 cups rolled oats
1 cup brown sugar
2 teaspoons baking powder
1 egg, beaten

Melt butter, add to dry ingredients. Add egg, mix well. Drop from from spoon one inch apart on greased cookie sheets. Bake 8 to 10 minutes at 350°. Let stand 1 minute, remove from pan.
Makes about 6 dozen.

Gazpacho

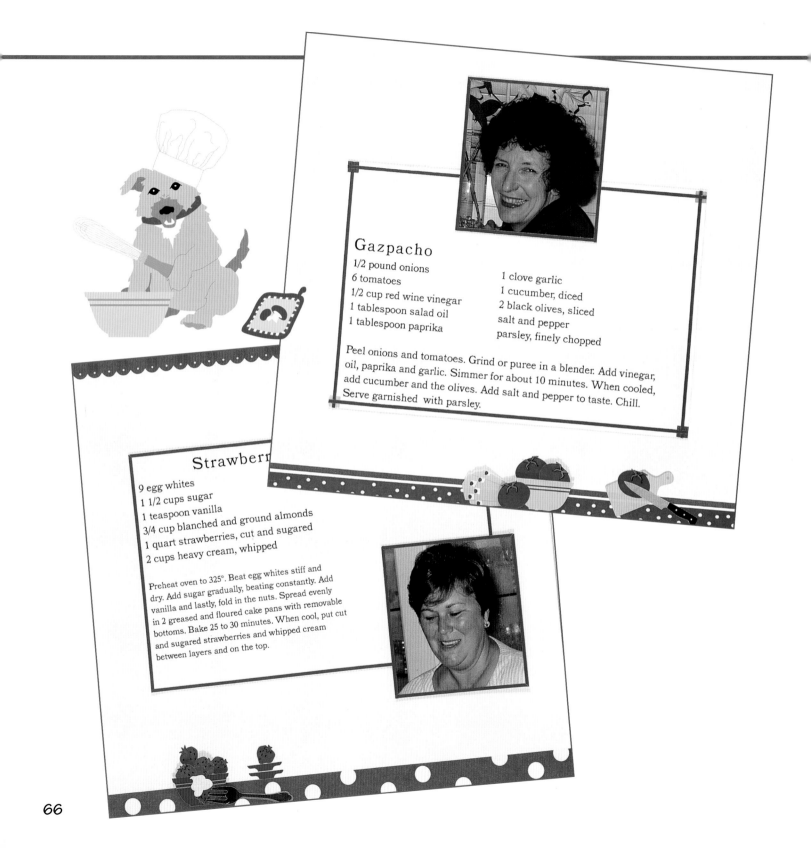

1/2 pound onions
6 tomatoes
1/2 cup red wine vinegar
1 tablespoon salad oil
1 tablespoon paprika
1 clove garlic
1 cucumber, diced
2 black olives, sliced
salt and pepper
parsley, finely chopped

Peel onions and tomatoes. Grind or puree in a blender. Add vinegar, oil, paprika and garlic. Simmer for about 10 minutes. When cooled, add cucumber and the olives. Add salt and pepper to taste. Chill. Serve garnished with parsley.

Strawberr

9 egg whites
1 1/2 cups sugar
1 teaspoon vanilla
3/4 cup blanched and ground almonds
1 quart strawberries, cut and sugared
2 cups heavy cream, whipped

Preheat oven to 325°. Beat egg whites stiff and dry. Add sugar gradually, beating constantly. Add vanilla and lastly, fold in the nuts. Spread evenly in 2 greased and floured cake pans with removable bottoms. Bake 25 to 30 minutes. When cool, put cut and sugared strawberries and whipped cream between layers and on the top.

Apple Pie

Filling:

6 to apples
1/2 cup sugar
1 Tbsp. butter
cinnamon, nutmeg, and lemon juice

Crust:

2 cups flour
1/2 tsp. salt
1/4 cup ice water
2/3 cup shortening

Sift flour and salt. Make paste of 1/3 cup of the four and water. Blend shortening into the remaining flour. Add paste. Stir well. Pare, core and slice apples. Line pie pan with pastry. Fill with sliced apples. Sprinkle with sugar and bits of the butter, spices and lemon juice. Slash and prick the upper crust. Lay upper crust on the top and pinch to make edges. Bake for 45 minutes to 1 hour at 425°.

... Vinaigrette

... tsp. salt
1/8 tsp. paprika
1/8 tsp. white pepper
1 1/2 Tb. tarragon vinegar
1 1/2 Tb. lemon juice
1 tsp. minced chives
1 tsp. flat leaf parsley
1 clove garlic pressed
6 Tb. olive oil

Using a wire whisk combine ingredients in the order given.

Travel

Israel

A major adventure was my first trip to Israel, begun when I was invited to join a group from my church. Our leader was a remarkable man who commands respect from everyone he touches. The trip was amazing and created great memories. At one stop, Beth Sha'en, I looked over an entire Roman city destroyed by an earthquake in 70 A.D. and I thought "Jason has to see this!" Two years later that wish came true. The album I made for Jason again demanded a simple, respectful treatment. I chose a 10"-square album with pages that matched the color of Israel. The book was made in 1996 and choices of albums and papers weren't as abundant as they are now. Still, I think the album is effective and we both love looking at it.

• Top: Whenever I travel, I look for heart-shaped rocks. Sometimes I miss a nice view, but I always come home with a rock or two. I attached one to the cover of the album.

• Left: By trimming paper and adding opal seashell stickers, I was able to suggest the shoreline of the Mediterranean Sea.

• Top: One of the fascinations in Israel is the contrast of ancient and contemporary eras. Here we are standing on the site of an ancient monastery surrounded by the signs of modern warfare. I penciled the guide line to write the journaling in brown ink.

• Left: The tall, narrow buildings required vertical photographs with people in them for scale.

• Right: I wanted to include this book on the Garden Tomb in the album, so I added the paper I had been using throughout, and slipped it into photo corners.

• Bottom: I don't do a lot of cropping (I like to crop in the camera), but I do like to use this technique to describe a detail, an action, etc. It requires patience and careful measuring. I used tracing paper to crop the photos and establish the mosaic look of the spread. With careful measuring and trimming, I accomplished my goal of highlighting the ancient ruins that Jason was so fascinated with. The vellum overlaps identify the spot and the passage in the Bible where it was mentioned.

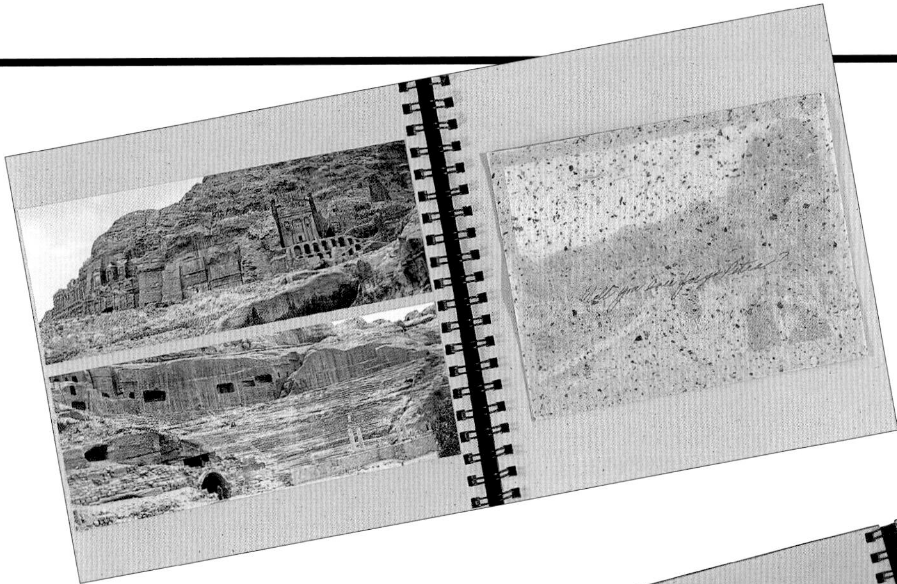

• This time, I chose to hide a very special photo under a fold of paper. Petra made a deep impression on Jason and me. The first glimpse of this incredible ancient city is breathtaking. So I highlighted that first view with a "curtain" of thin, handmade paper that had a feel of the stone surroundings from which this city was carved. I attached a portion of the paper to the back of the photo before I mounted it on the page.

• Top left: Jason was put off by the crowds of people in Jerusalem, so to demonstrate his discomfort I put all the photos at an angle—something I do not ordinarily do.

• Top right: To chronicle our reactions to Jerusalem, I put a journaling panel under a folded piece of paper.

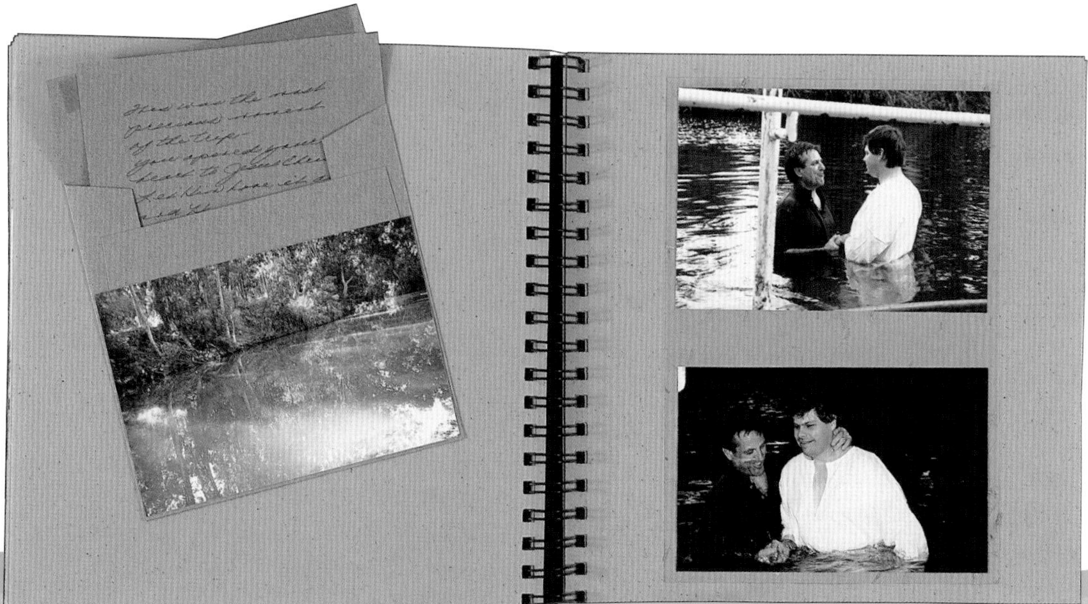

• Left: To express my feelings about Jason's baptism, I enclosed a personal note in an envelope made with just the "right" color paper for the page.

Columbia River Cruise Album

I have had other memorable trips, all made noteworthy by my traveling companions.

In 2001, my brother Bertin and his wife Muriel invited my nephew Greg, his 15-year old-son Bradley, and me on a trip commemorating Lewis and Clark. To top off the great team, Bertin and Muriel brought their grandson Tyler, Brad's cousin.

We traveled along the Columbia, Snake, and Willamette Rivers on a beautiful old sternwheeler, the Queen of the West. I gave an album to Greg for his birthday and a small thank-you album to Bertin and Muriel.

• Opposite; For Greg, I chose a blue album and used a riverboat sticker back-to-back for the title page. This provided me with the perfect journaling panel and hid our embarkation photo. Since the boat was festooned in American flags, I took the opportunity to embellish it with Design Lines and flag stickers. I also used tiny printed papers in red, white, and blue for accents.

• Top: I cut down the right edge of the page slightly so that a confetti heart could be added. Then I backed it with one in green on the following page.

• Bottom: The added fly sheet of blue vellum announces the first stop on our journey. Blue alphabet stickers worked with the cover for titles throughout the book.

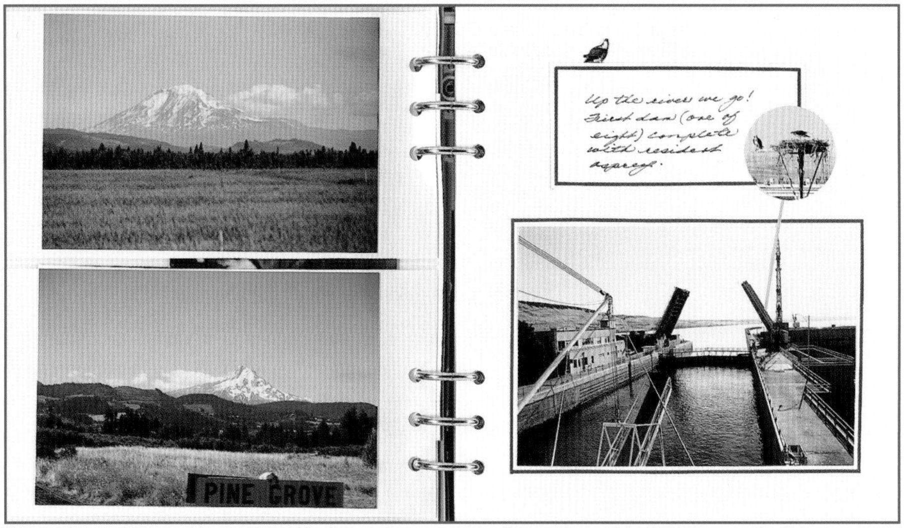

• Left: I punched a close-up of the bird's nest on the lock and added a Design Line "sliver" to show the location of the nest. Another copy of the bird, cut in silhouette, accents the journaling panel.

• Bottom: I used spicy zigzag Design Lines to embellish the photos of our visit with the Tamastslikt Indians in Pendleton.

• Because I like to follow a theme, I often repeat throughout an album. In this case, it is the technique of two photos on a small inserted page.

• The boys made our trip. I had to take pictures of them being boys, so they would have their own commemorative pages. Look for opportunities to take candid photos of your traveling companions. They will add color and humor to your story. I cut down the right sides of the pages and added small flag stickers back-to-back to delineate the onboard activities pages.

• The casual alphabet title of this page follows the flow of the water Design Line at the bottom of the page.

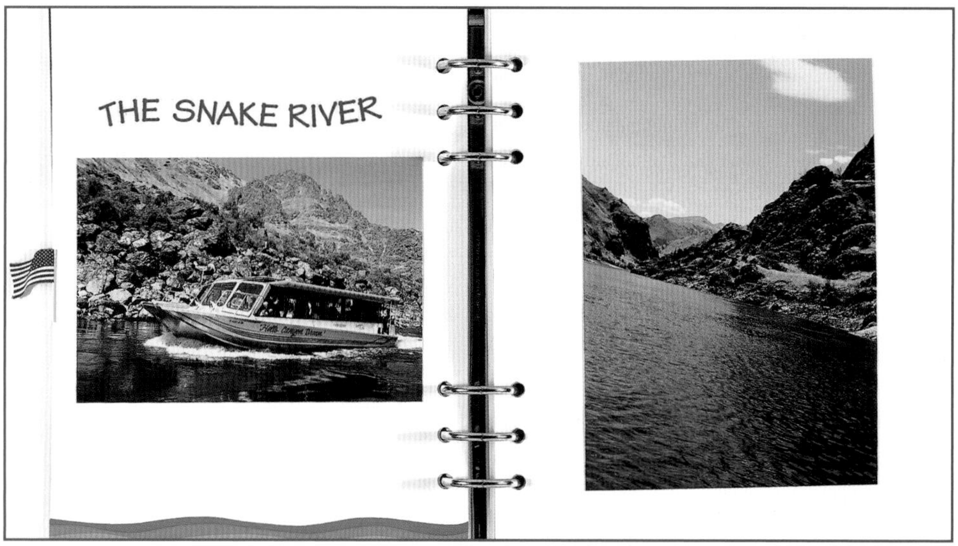

• I created the medallion by adding a small piece cut from one of the album pages, outlined in a red sliver stickers. A rabbit coming out of the hat repeated the magic theme of the evening's show. The journaling panels are decorated with concerto Design Lines.

• I added this page because the paper reminded me of the texture of the cement locks. I decorated the page with a ship's wheel, referencing the riverboat.

• When I'm in a location with a dramatic vista, I like to stand in one spot and take pictures of the horizon, section by section, carefully keeping my camera level. Mt. St. Helens certainly gave me that opportunity! Once the pictures were developed, I created an accordion-fold to show off the scene. I then cut the pages to fit the photos, attached the pages together with book tape, and then mounted the photo. If you plan to do this technique, take photos for the back panels of the pages.

• I used a trimmed-down page to act as a two-sided journaling panel and to add a little interest.

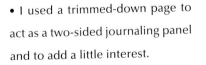

• I made a matching paper pocket to hold several more mementos, then tied on the luggage tags to finish the album off.

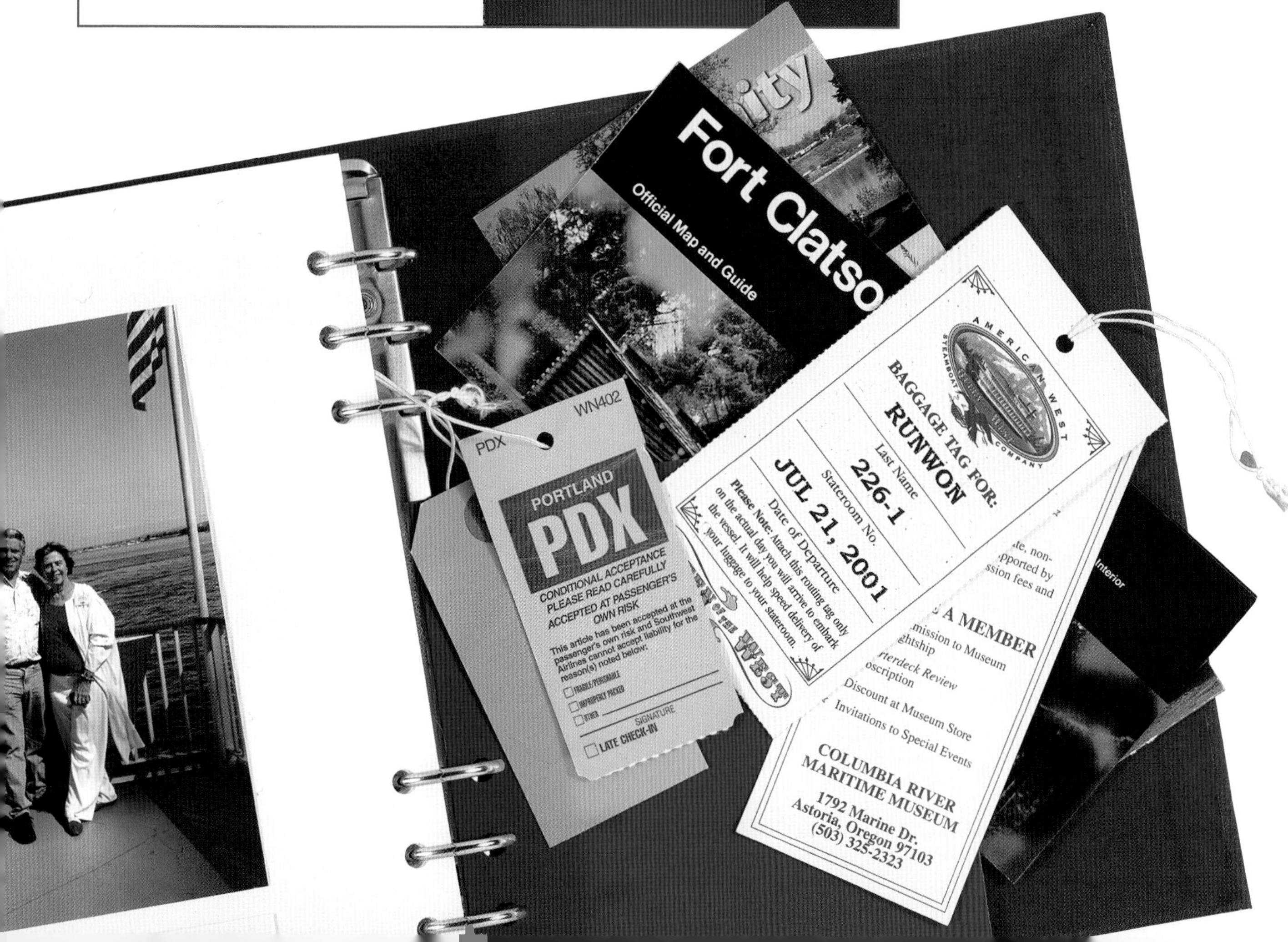

Columbia River Thank-you Album

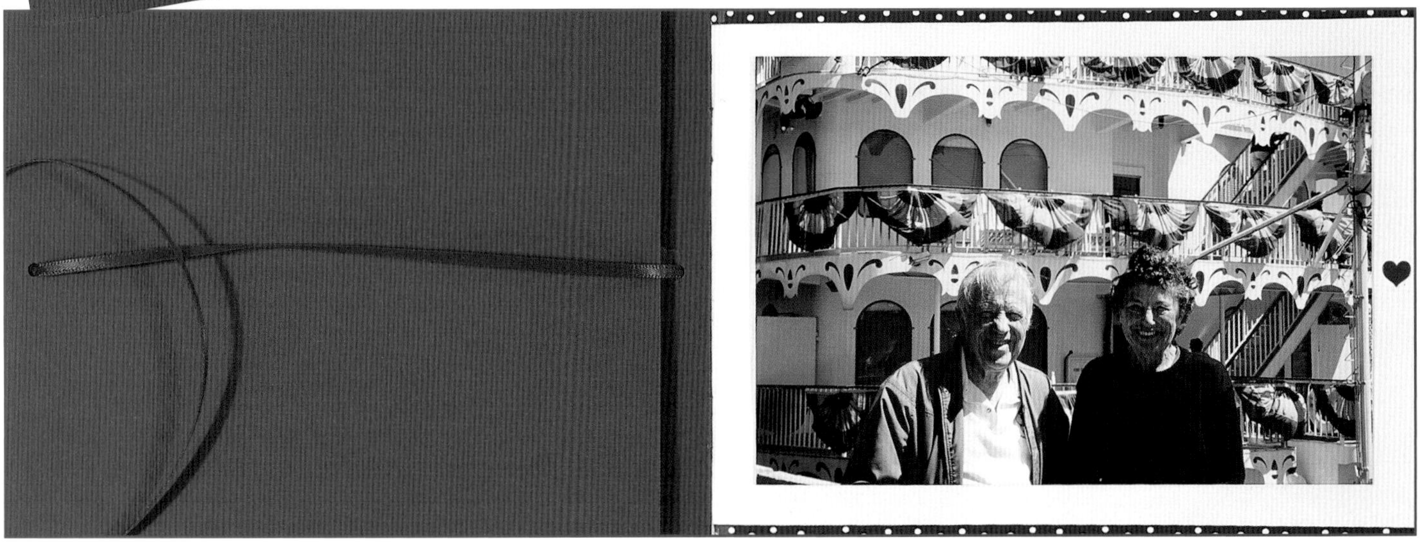

My brother Bertin included me on the Columbia River cruise. In order to thank him, I created this little album. I used a royal blue album with red ribbon to go with the patriotic theme of the boat.

I included the best photos I had taken of Bertin and his wife Muriel, and a few of the highlights of the trip to remind him of all the special places we visited and the fun we had.

• Top: Near the end of this album, I repeated the same panorama foldout that I made for the Columbia River Cruise album.

• Bottom: I wrote my thank-you's on a card and glued it on the inside back cover.

Bertie and Muriel, you have
given us a memory to last for
a lifetime. It was brilliant
to bring the boys, because
they made the trip. Thank
you once again for a
perfectly planned trip and
a red, white and blue bang-up
good time. I love you. Peg

Greece

Greece was another memorable trip. Jason, Kim, and I traveled with Prison Fellowship through the Mediterranean and Aegean Seas, following Paul's journeys.

The trip was rich with new sights and learning. We had so many surprises that I tried to capture that feeling in creating the album. It was actually meant to be a "practice" album, but I liked it well enough to make it the album for that trip.

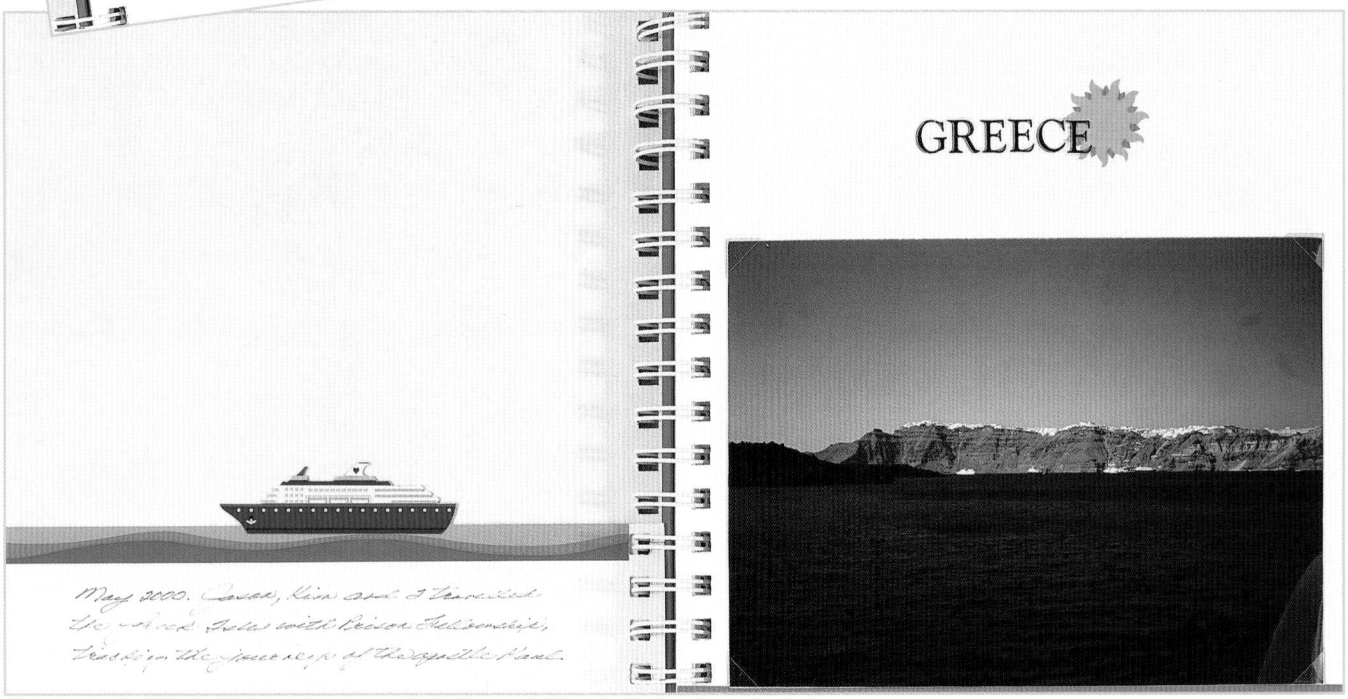

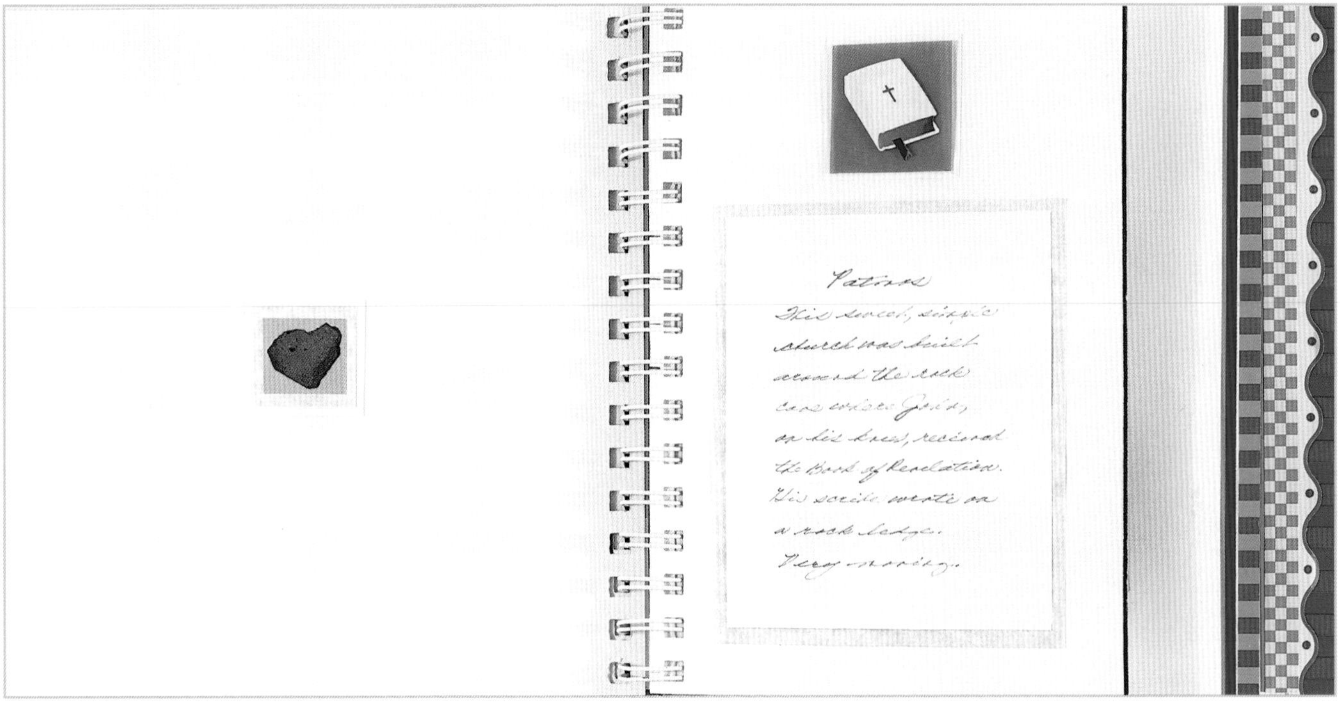

• The color choices were simple: clear blue, white, and stone. These are the colors of Greece. Our 8"-square blue spiral photo journal was perfect. Notice that the color you choose for your album will always frame the pages within.

• Opposite: For the title page, I enlarged a photo of Santorini and mounted it on the second page, with blue Design Lines top and bottom. When I have especially wonderful photos that I may want to use elsewhere, I attach them with clear photo corners so they can be easily removed. By cutting down the first page to just the right size for a cruise ship sticker to be cruising through the Mediterranean, I was able to title the book using only stickers. The reverse has a matching water Design Line, a matching ship, stuck back-to-back, and the journaling.

• Top: The photo of a heart-shaped stone from the Acropolis (I always collect heart-shaped stones in my travels) is mounted on two squares of matching white paper.

• I love to use "graduated pages" in order to have a splash of color at the beginning of the section. As you turn each page you get a new surprise and a slightly different look. To make the series of graduated pages, you will want to plan how many pages you want in that story section. Start with the back page of the group. Put on the edge trim that you want to have show from the beginning of the section. Cut the page in front of it to fit against the back page border. Apply the border to that page. Now trim the next to last page. Continue this system, moving toward the front page.

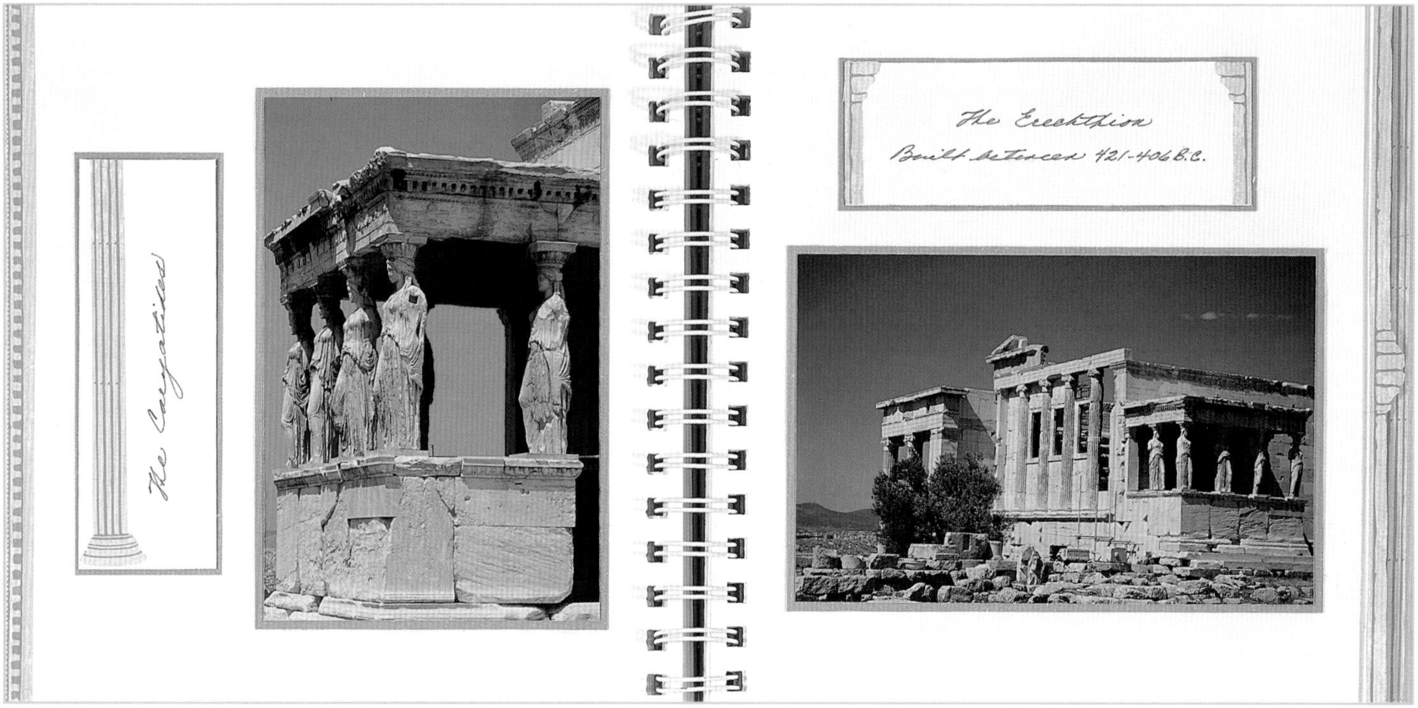

The Caryatides
The Erechthion
Built between 421-406 B.C.

• These photos inspired our art department to create Greek column stickers, and I used them to create another small graduated page segment. By cutting them, I created journaling panels, using a matching paper to mat photos as well.

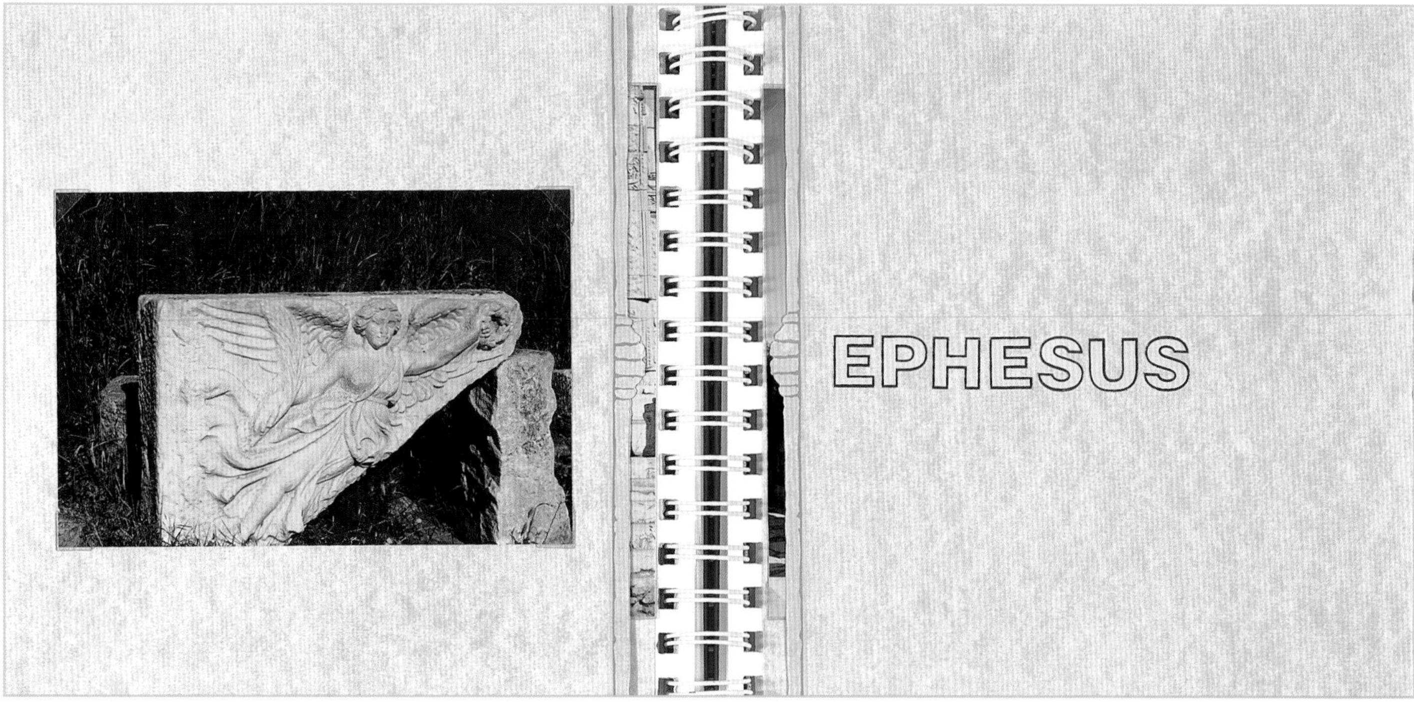

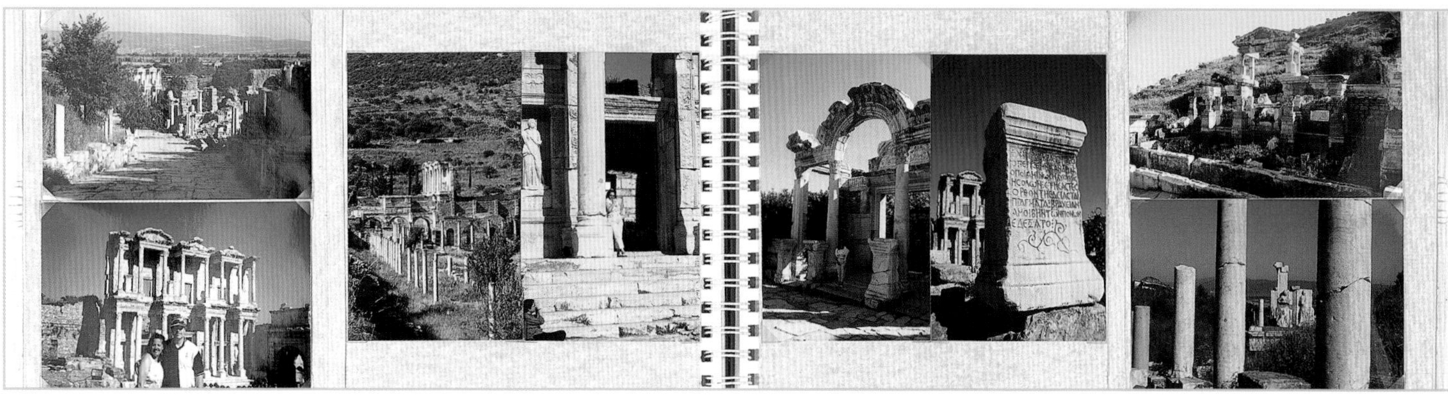

• Here I have repeated that wonderful marbleized paper from my first pages. It was fun finding new ways to use the column stickers.

• Ephesus demanded a dramatic treatment because it is a dramatic place. I used artist's tape, then cut strips of matching paper to cover the white tape. I also covered the whole page with the marbleized paper. By mounting photos flush against one another, I was able to get two 4" photos on a page and also capture some of the drama.

• Continuing the blue accents in mats and on journaling panels, I also used spice stickers where added in the medallions to complement the colors and themes of the photos.

• The "Friends" section was made to highlight special friendships we developed on the cruise. It was made by cutting one page of the book to 4 1/4"x6 1/4", big enough to cover the photo underneath. The photos underneath were placed to be exactly covered by the new small page. The title was added and finally the blue slivers on the edge.

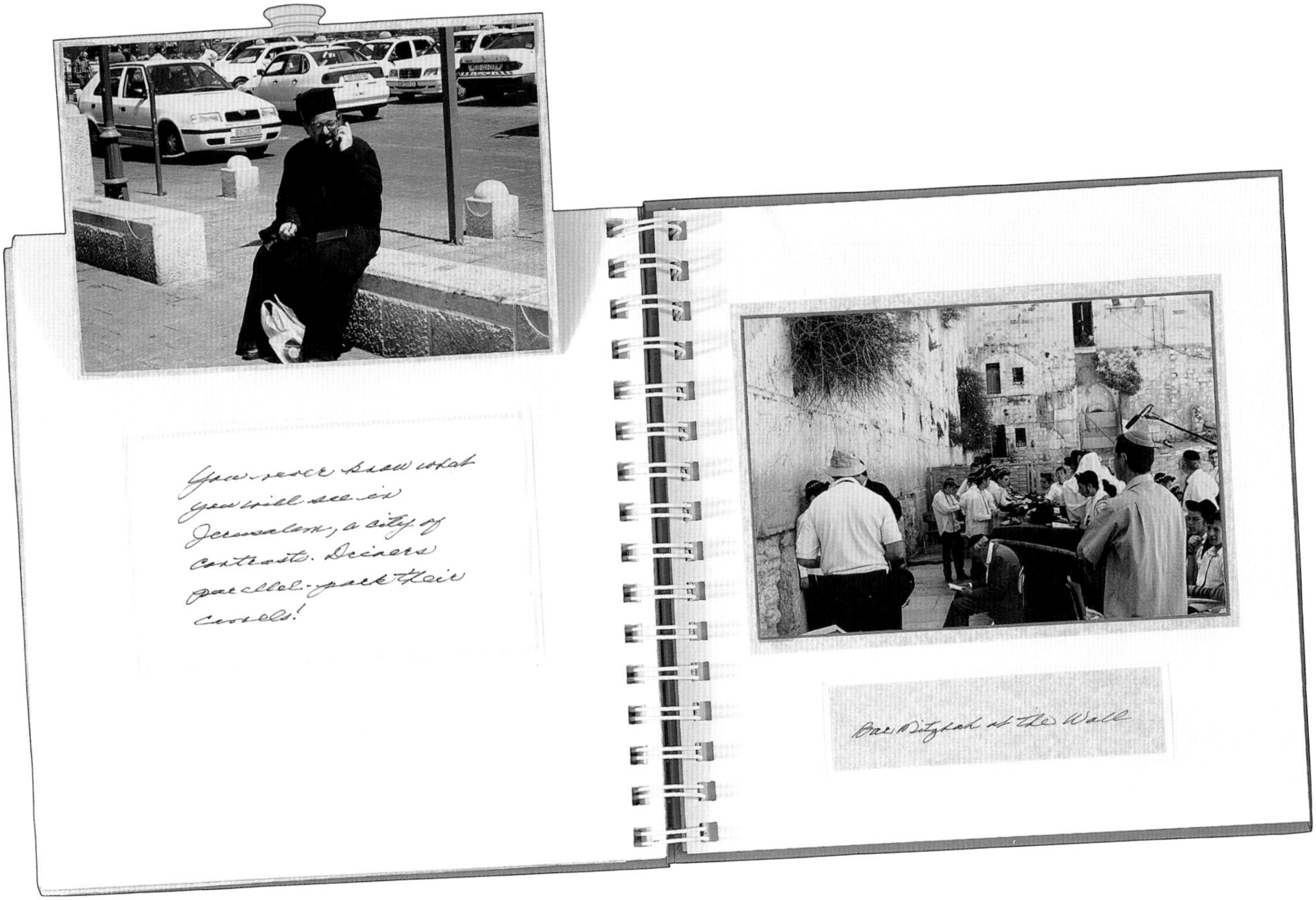

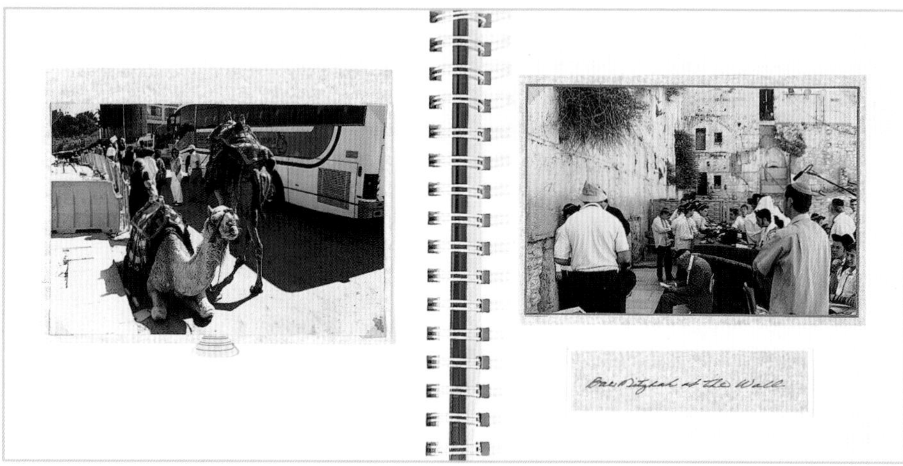

• In Jerusalem, you see the strangest sights. I tried to capture that idea by making a flip-up page contrasting the parallel-parked camel with the priest on a cell phone. I cut the stone paper with an 1/8" border, bottom, and sides, and 1/2" on top. Then I mounted the photos front and inside, scored the paper for the fold, and attached it to the page.

• I tore the paper for this mat to repeat the ragged edges of the rock surrounding the tomb.

Alaska

In 2002, I was invited to accompany Michele Gerbrandt, of *Memory Makers Magazine*, on a scrapbooking cruise to Alaska. I was so excited that I invited my nephew Greg and his son Bradley to join me. Knowing how much Greg had enjoyed his photo album from our last trip, I knew I would make another; so I began to take pictures as soon as we met in Vancouver. I chose an album that contained both plain scrapbooking pages as well as photo sleeves. By creating title pages, I was able to capture the essence of various parts of the trip; then I could simply slip in the photos, after the title page pertaining to that specific area. This resulted in less time spent decorating pages and a less fussy "man's" book. You will notice that there is no journaling. That will be Greg's contribution—his own reflections.

• Opposite, left; One of the things I love about this type of album is the little window on the cover. It gives me a chance to preview things to come. For this one, I chose a shot of Brad with our ship in the background and used gold alphabet stickers for the title.

• Opposite, right; I love this photo of Greg taken on the balcony outside his stateroom, because it said so much about how often we just stood quietly absorbing the beauty that was around us. Because this was the first page, I added a sliding panel with a pull tab for a quick preview of all of our activities. By gluing two pages together, leaving an opening for the sliding panel, I created a pocket. I cut the panel in a T-shape that keeps it from sliding competely out of the book.

• Top: This was my first title page. I matted the photo of the bald eagle we saw in downtown Juneau with rainbow vellum Design Lines, and added a celery vellum alphabet. An eagle sticker added to a vellum medallion finished it off.

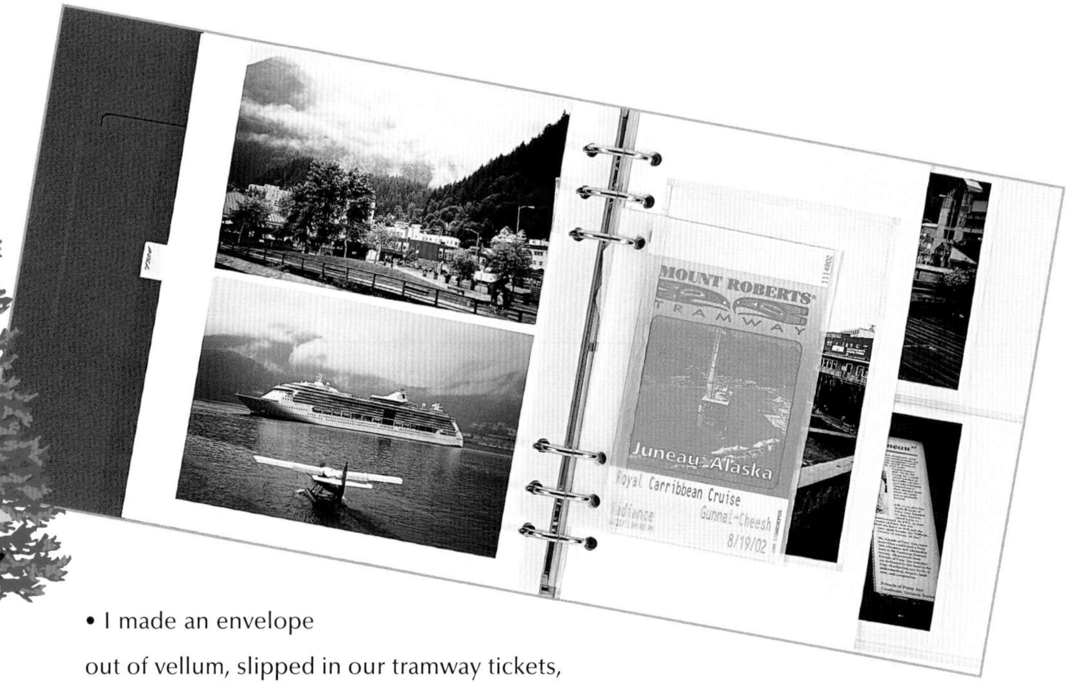

• I made an envelope out of vellum, slipped in our tramway tickets, punched it, and added it to the album. I always save as many souvenirs as possible because they add some interest to an album. It's fun to see more than photos—just another way to tell the story.

• Because this album is friendlier to horizontal photos, I took an opportunity to add a couple of verticals by cutting down one of the scrapbook pages. I like to use an element of surprise to add interest.

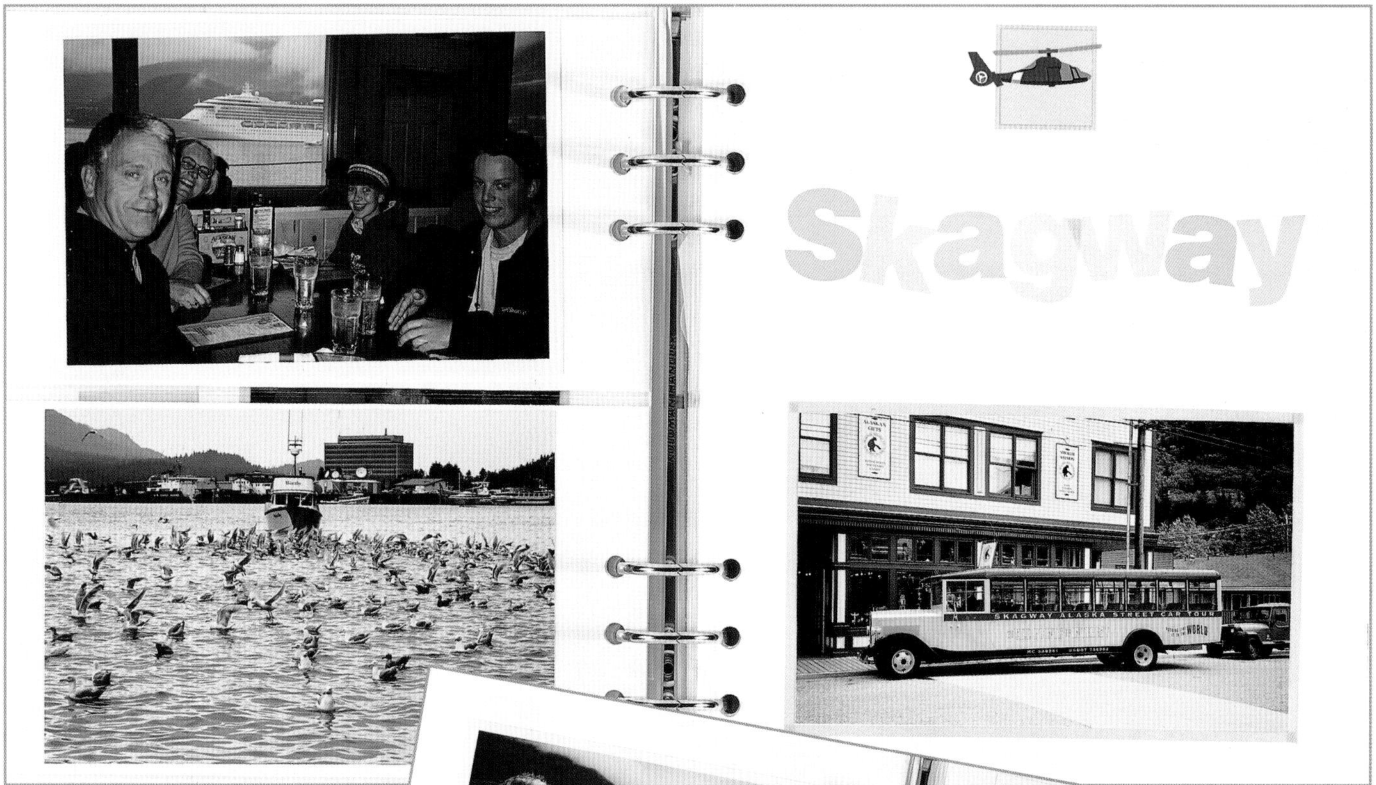

• On to Skagway, where I used the same technique for a title page, changing colors and accents to match our activities.

• This great adventures train sticker almost matched the one we rode up the mountain.

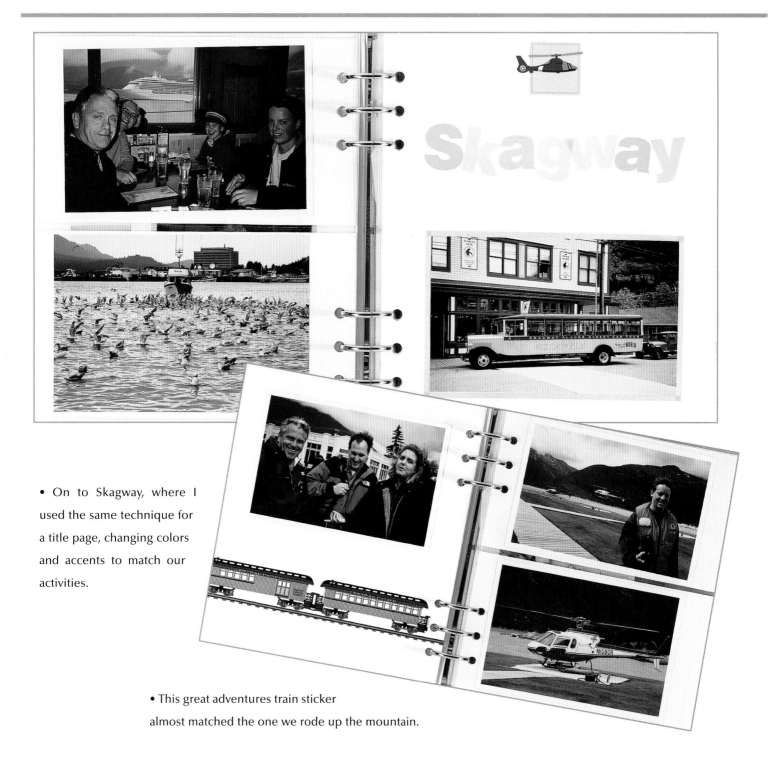

• The thrill of our trip was a helicopter ride to a glacier. I combined two pages, using a textile print vellum Design Line to attach the two pages.

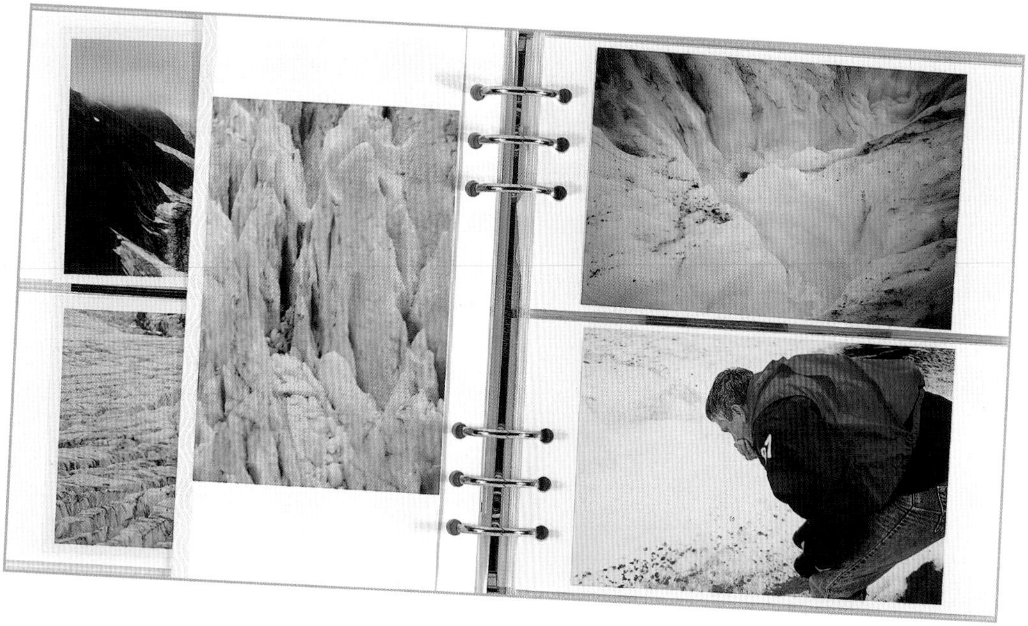

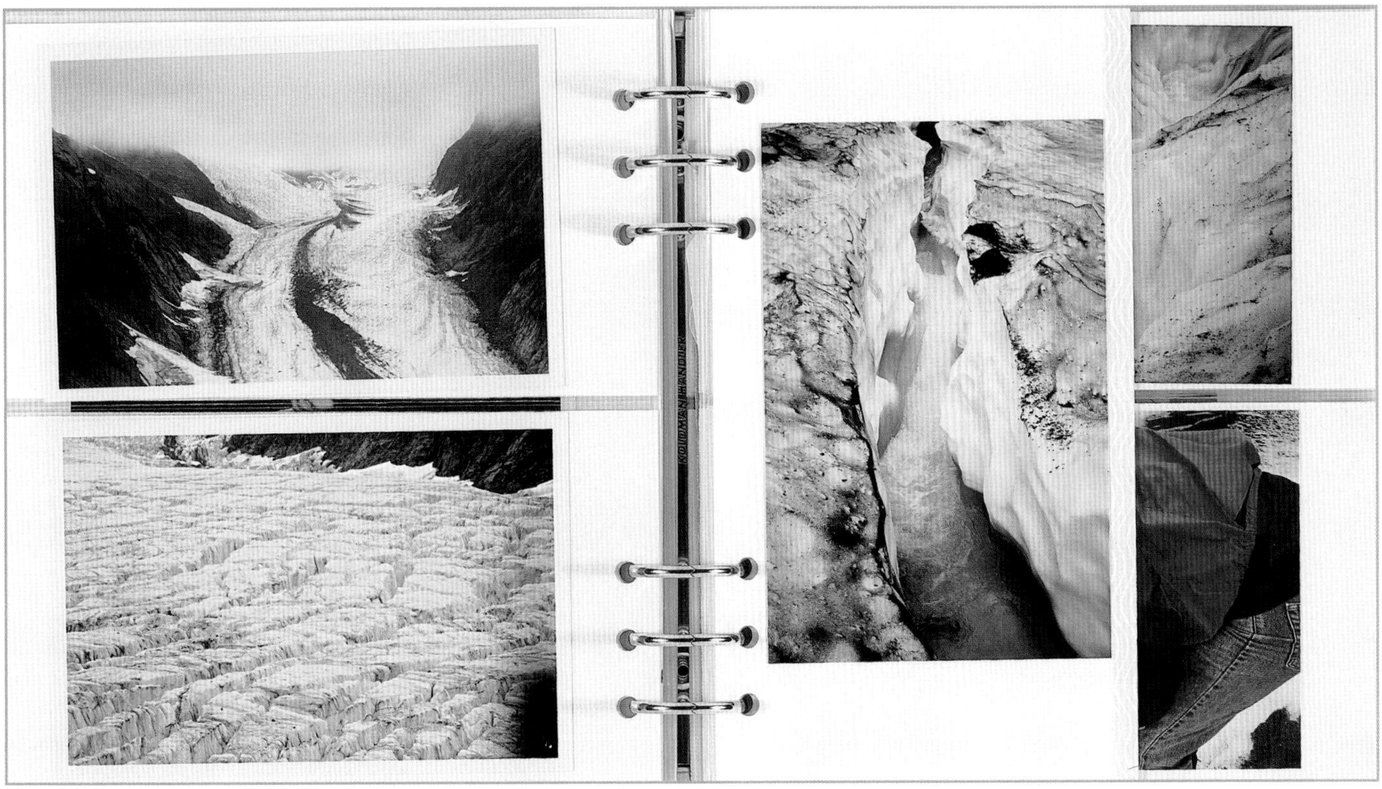

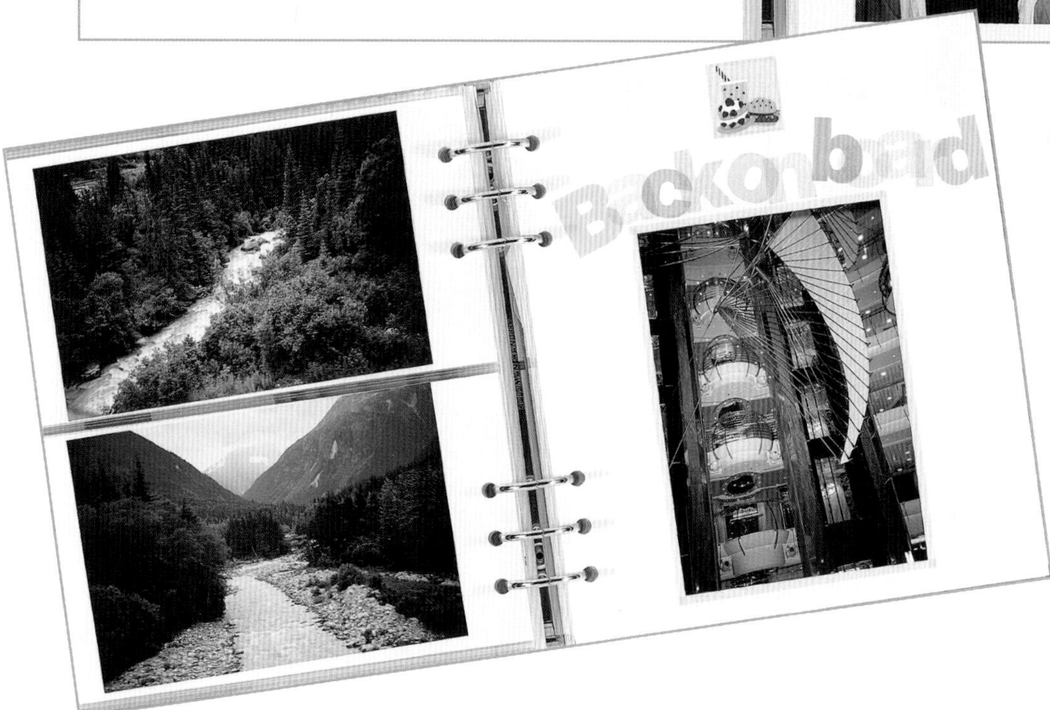

• I repeated the format for all of the title pages. However, I made some adjustments for each topic. This gave me a chance to do one of my favorite things—combine several colors of the vellum alphabet stickers. I love the way the colors work together and how they create new colors by overlapping. It looks easy, but I spent time carefully selecting the shades for each letter.

• It poured the day we went to Ketchikan, so I was able to make great use of clouds and raindrops stickers.

• My final page! Luggage tags were in our staterooms so that suitcases could be taken out by midnight. I kept extra tags and picked up the theme for my last title page. It just seemed natural to punch a hole in the tags and attach them onto one of the binder rings.

Antarctica

Here's an example of how my life is blessed:

My friends Luci Swindoll and Mary Graham, Women of Faith, were visiting our offices in mid-November of 2002 and told me they were going to Antarctica in two weeks. I told them I was excited for them because I had always wanted to go, and they quickly said, "Why don't you come with us?" My son came into the room later, and I asked him, "Jason, where have I always wanted to go?" and he replied without a moment's hesitation, "Antarctica." Mary, and my noble assistant Sherryl moved heaven and earth to cancel a videotaping, get reservations, and schedule a personal shopper to gather the clothes and gear I needed. Friends at church took over the leadership of the Angel Tree program (a big task) and within 13 days I was on my way to living a dream.

I read *Endurance* by Ernest Lansing twenty years ago, and it gave me a deep yearning to see Antarctica. Even though I gave the book to several traveling buddies, I couldn't interest anyone in going there with me. Most people said, "Why would you want to go there?"

• The basic colors of this incredible place are blue, white, dark brown, and black (which the penguins supply). Because it is so strikingly simple, I felt it asked for a simple treatment. I chose silver to capture the feeling of all that ice, and the silver glint off the water. I chose red because our parkas and so many of the accents on the ship were red. I cut plain black journaling panels to use with my silver pen.

• My limited accessories included vellum papers in clear, light blue, leaf green, and silver; red and black card stocks; and stickers: metallic "sliver" Design Lines (lots of them!), penguins, reflection snowflakes, lustre hearts.

• I took many photos through the porthole of my cabin. So to symbolize the journey, I added a porthole to this photo of penguins. The postcard is one I mailed from the only post office in Antarctica. I used ribbon that was on our luggage tag to hold a letter written on vellum with a look of snow. The letter told the story of how I came to be on the trip.

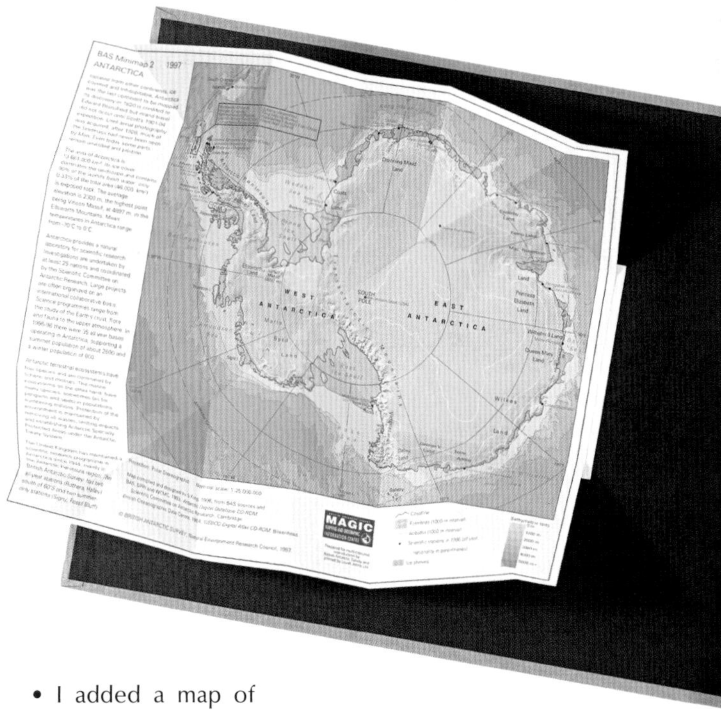

• I added a map of Antarctica on the inside of the cover. I love the way it pops out and serves as a perfect reference.

• All journaling in the album was done on black paper with a silver pen. The pencil guidelines were erased, then the paper was trimmed to uniform size and mounted on the pages.

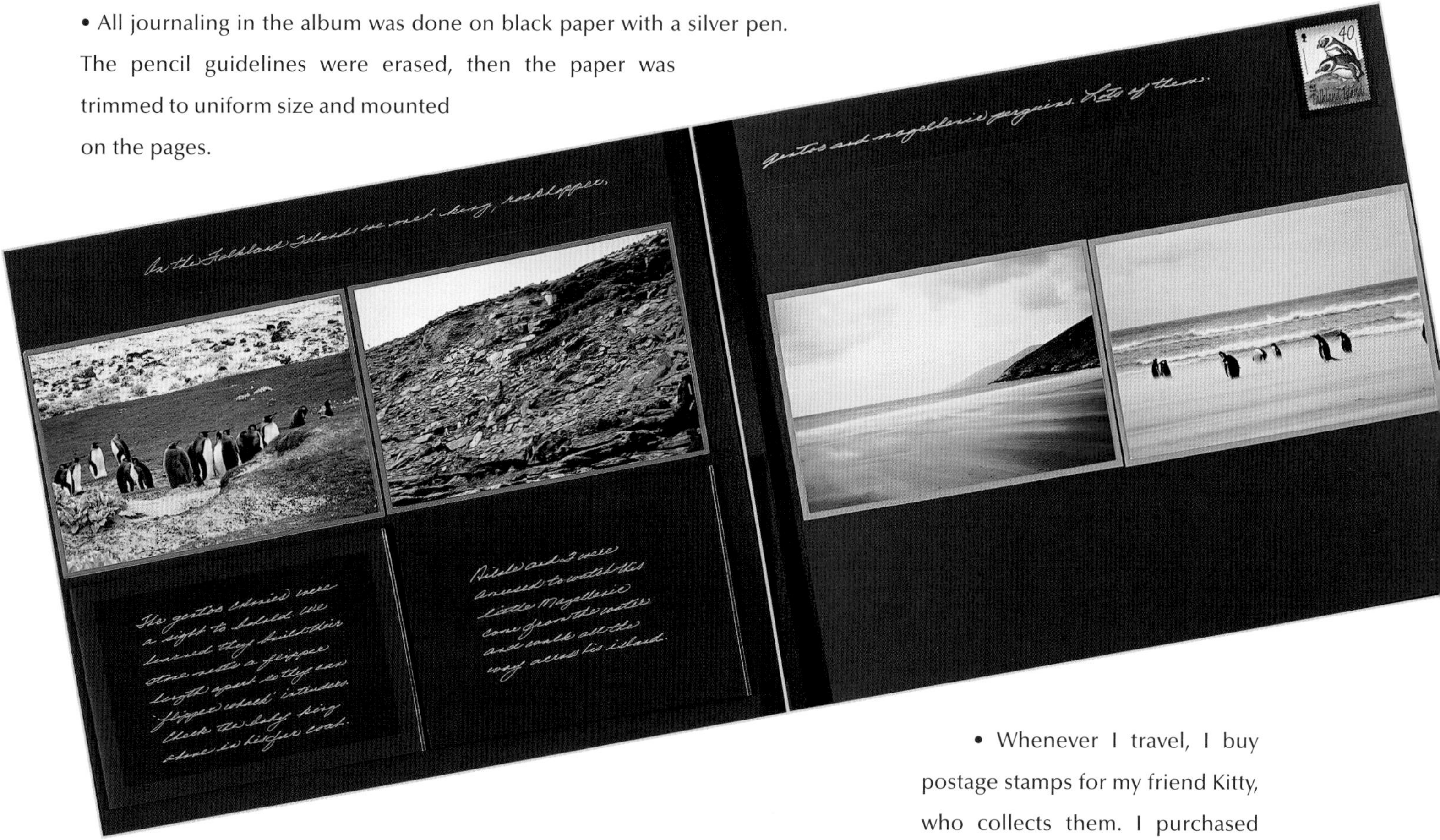

• Whenever I travel, I buy postage stamps for my friend Kitty, who collects them. I purchased extras for myself in the Falklands and thought this was the perfect place to highlight one.

• The album of the trip was a challenge. White paper washed out the photos and ivory clashed. It had to be black paper. Antarctica is a big place and a massive subject. I chose an 11"x14" gray album with a little window on the cover.

• Starting here and throughout the book, I used silver "sliver" Design Lines to indicate that additional pictures were to be found behind the silver line.

• To make foldout panels, like the one for the Falkland Islands, cut 4"x6" panels from card stock and hinge them together with bookbinding tape (available from some art stores or special craft stores). Mount your photos, making certain you give space for the foldout to close.

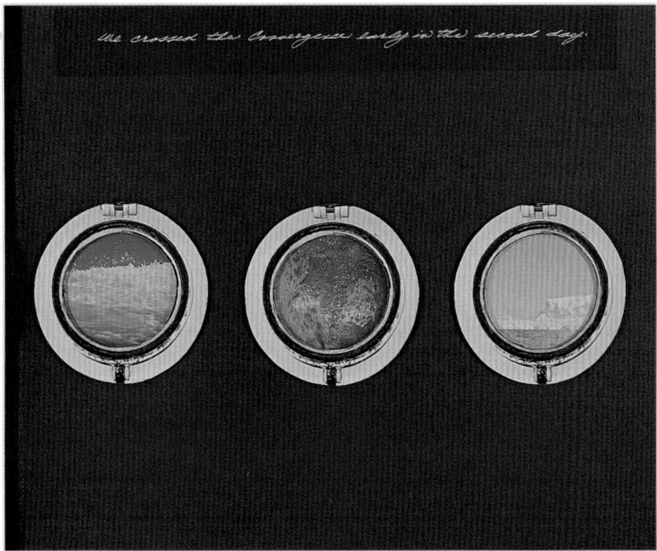

• To use the technique on the Drake Passage pages, order multiple prints of the "framing" photo (a door, window, or porthole) and carefully crop out the interiors. Then cut the "view" prints to fit under the frames. You might need to blacken the inside edges of the frame if the cut is obvious. On this series, I raised the portholes with mounting tape for effect.

• The "peek-a-boo" technique on the bottom right of the Elephant Island pages is simple. Back the cover print with desired colored paper, leaving 3/8"–1/2" of paper at the top. Fold the extra paper back behind the photo to create a small flap. Before you mount the "hidden picture" on the page, open the flap. Mount pictures on the inside, if desired.

• To make a mosaic of similar photos, cut a window from card stock or draw one on tracing paper to decide where you want to crop your photos. Carefully mark the photos, then cut accurately. They can touch one another, or you can leave 1/16" margins between them.

• To make the flip pages for "What Penguins Do All Day", cut four pieces of paper 12"x6 1/4" and place them in a stack vertically. Stagger the ends of the paper closest to you, so that they are about 1/4" apart. Paper-clip either side of the stack to keep the spacing from shifting. Then carefully fold the top half of the stack down so that it is 1/4" away from the end of the top page. Remove paper clips and separate pages. Use a burnisher or bone folder along each crease to make pages lay down flat. Place pages back together again. Then unfold flip book and use a hole punch to make holes along the crease (1" from either edge of the crease and one directly in the middle).

• To bind the flip book together, use a generous length of ribbon or heavy thread. Starting from the back, bring the thread through the center hole to the inside. Now go across and take the thread through the left hole to the back, across the back to the right hole, through the right hole to the front and across to the center, and through the center hole again to the back. Finish by tying the thread in a knot or bow.

• This journaling technique is done by making vellum sleeves 1/4" larger than the photos that are mounted on them. The journaling panels are cut smaller and the red and blue tags (with my

311
Zodiac procedures
After taking 20
minutes to gear
up we go below
to the launch
area. We turn
our tag (room
number) from
blue to red and
BLUE ON BOARD
ASHORE

m number on them) are punched with a 1 1/2" punch, then nched with a 1/8" hole. The penguin sticker commemorates first "landing."

311
excursion is
over we board
the ship and
scrub our boots
in antiseptic
solution, so as
not to carry disease

• The iceberg spread is done with extra pages from the album. Trim the outside edge so that the pages don't reach all the way into the spine of the album—you need space so they won't interfere with closing. Hinge with bookbinding tape on the outside first, then on the inside.

• To accent the gorgeous colors of the sunset (and the hidden sunrise from the other side of the ship) I chose rose metallic "sliver" Design Lines.

• To make the pocket for the postcards, make a rectangle with 1/4" folding flaps on all four sides. Make the lowest horizontal slit about 1/4 the length of the postcard up from the bottom of the pocket. Allowing 3/4" in between, cut as many additional slits as needed. Each slit is approximately 1/16" wide. Fold the tabs under and attach the pocket to a rectangle that is 1/4" larger in each direction. Add a red mat and attach to the page.

• To make the postage stamp, trim a photo to the desired size, mat on white paper. Then trim the edges with the "postage stamp" paper trimmers.

Enough said!

Faith

Count your blessings

Angola Prison Album & Document Folder

People often ask me why I continue to visit prisoners. I can only respond by saying, "You just have to experience it to understand it." I have been moved by the incredible ministry of Prison Fellowship, so when I was invited to visit a prison, I accepted the opportunity. To touch people who are in such desperate need and to give them a message of hope is a very rewarding experience. Anyone who is involved in ministry will tell you they receive far more than they give, and that is certainly true.

In 2002, I was invited to visit Angola Prison in Louisiana on Easter weekend with my friend Chuck Colson. I was a tad apprehensive because of the prison's reputation, but I couldn't miss the opportunity. What I witnessed there has made an indelible impression. The prison, which was a slave farm before the Civil War, had a history of cruelty and violence. It was considered the toughest prison in the United States. Eight years ago, Burl Cain became the warden of this 18,000-acre facility and has transformed it into a productive farm and an almost self-sustaining operation. The inmates I met spoke of the peace that covers the entire place.

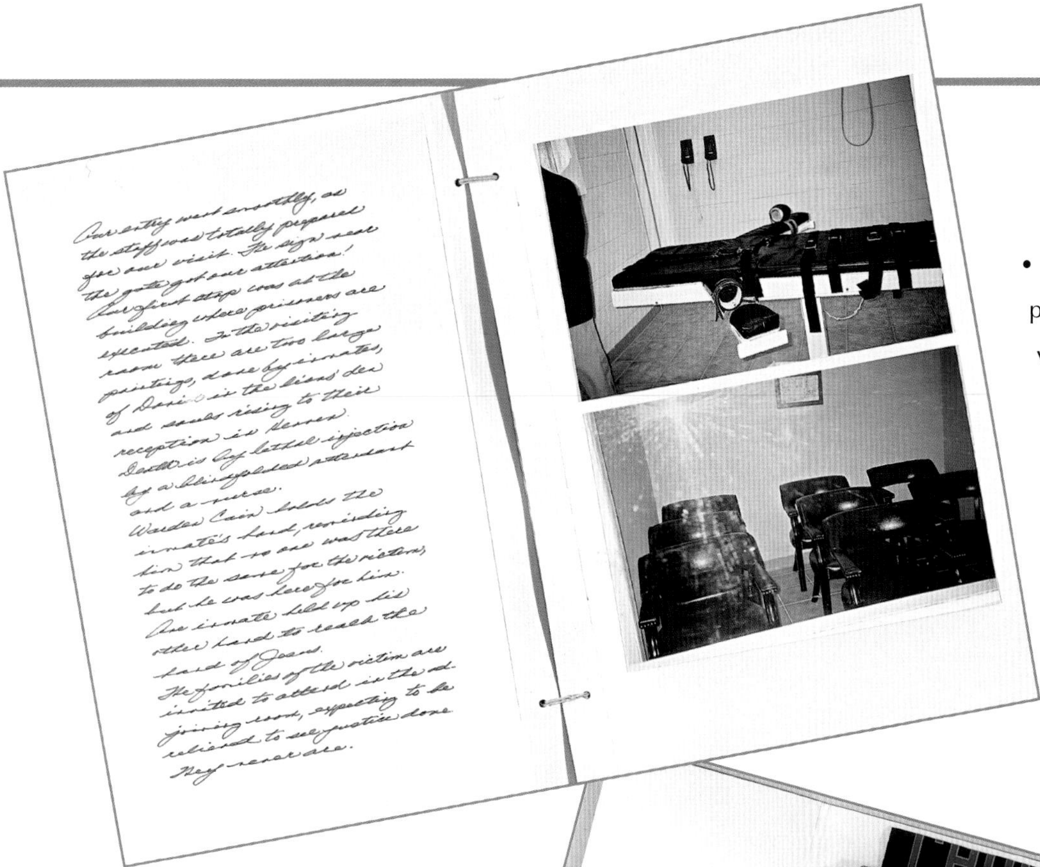

• The book was made with light gray paper and the journaling was written on vellum and tipped in. The silver vellum cover is titled with our laser-cut alphabet stickers. The binding, a clever idea from one of our artists, Tami Lovett, was made with wire twisted to resemble barbed wire and held in place through the holes in the pages with rubber bands.

I had to record my feelings and the story of this amazing transformation. It is a personal document made just to keep the memory fresh and to share with others. I gathered quite a few pieces during that weekend and some after, so I made a document folder to hold them.

• To make the document folder, I cut and scored heavy card stock to fit my collection of memorabilia, then bound it with a band of matching paper. For the title, I used the lettering to match the album.

Count Your Blessings Album

I often reflect upon my many blessings, thanking the Lord for them every day. I have so many, that I often forget to mention them all. Like a prayer journal, I thought it would be a good idea to record these blessings and review them regularly, adding new ones as they occur. It has been a lovely exercise and I've become quite attached to the book. When you reflect upon all your many blessings, it helps to get you through the tough times, and to realize during those times that things will turn around, and more blessings are just around the corner.

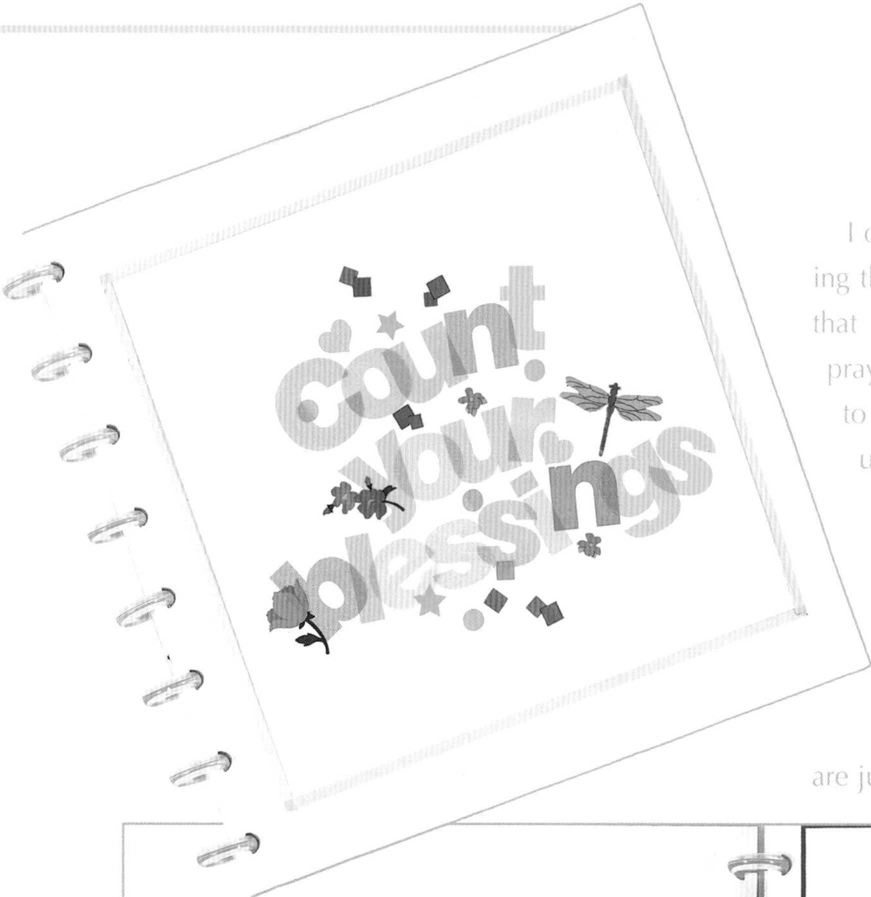

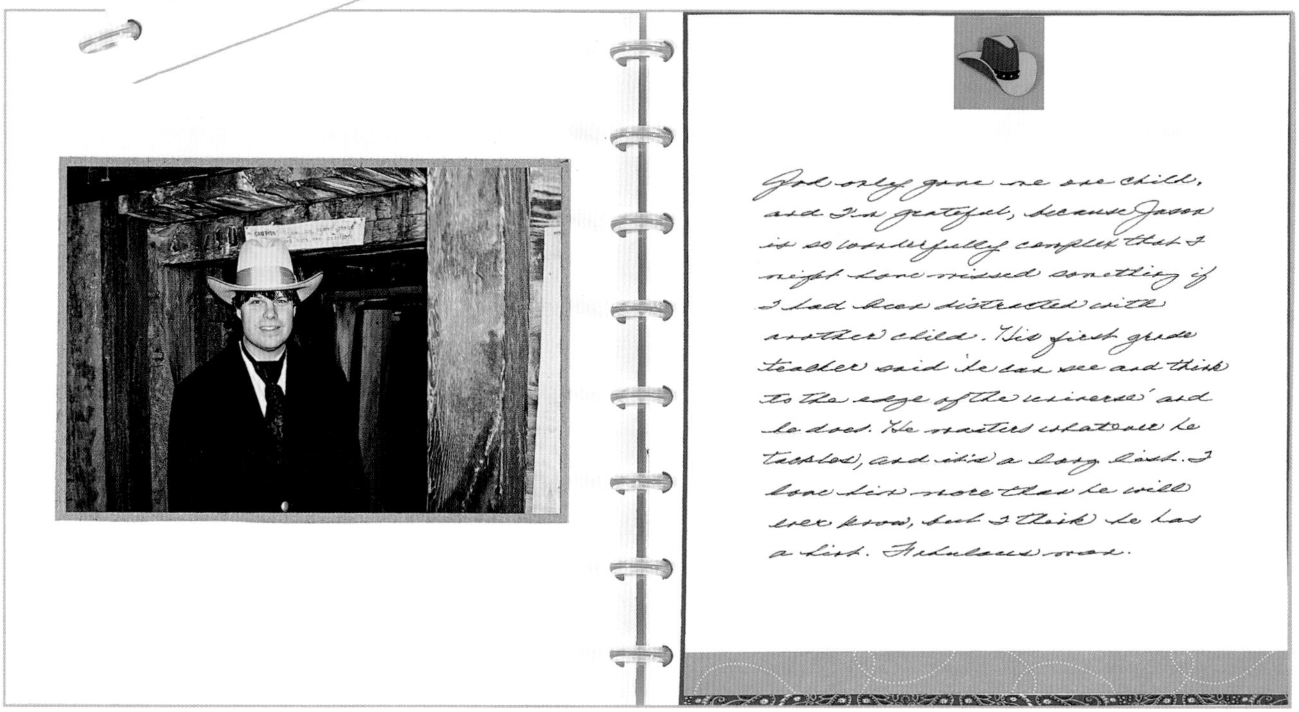

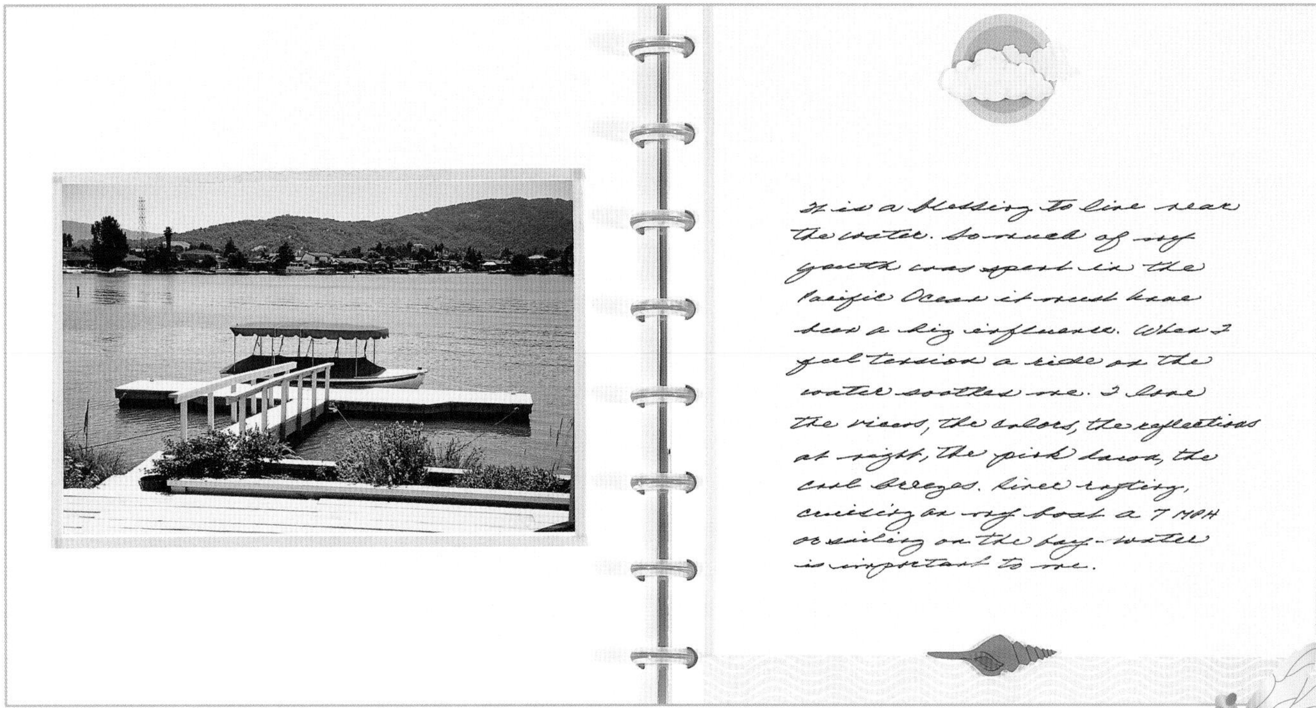

It is a blessing to live near
the water. So much of my
youth was spent in the
Pacific Ocean it must have
been a big influence. When I
feel tension a ride on the
water soothes me. I love
the views, the colors, the reflections
at night, the pink dawn, the
cool breezes. River rafting,
cruising on my boat a 7 MPH
or sailing on the bay - water
is important to me.

71
My home is my sanctuary.
I am blessed to live in a
house on the water, one
flooded with light. Every hour
of the day offers a new beauty.
I chose pale colors and simple art:
people are the decor. Serene and
tranquil, people often drop their
tensions when they enter. It is
a blessing I love to share.

When Corrie ten Boom and her sister were imprisoned in a Nazi concentration camp, they made a regular practice of counting their blessings. They were often harassed and mistreated by their captors and their quarters even became infested with fleas. One day they noticed the soldiers weren't coming around very often and found out they were annoyed by the fleas. Immediately they added fleas to their blessings!

I didn't want another dog
after I lost Max – it's just
too hard. But after a while I
began feeling too selfish – I needed
to have someone to love and take
care of. Perfect timing: Rogers had
just sired his second litter.
Beau has blessed me with his
sweet disposition and loving
nature. "Want to go?" is his favorite
word, and we do it a lot. What
other dog knows the word "snuggle"?

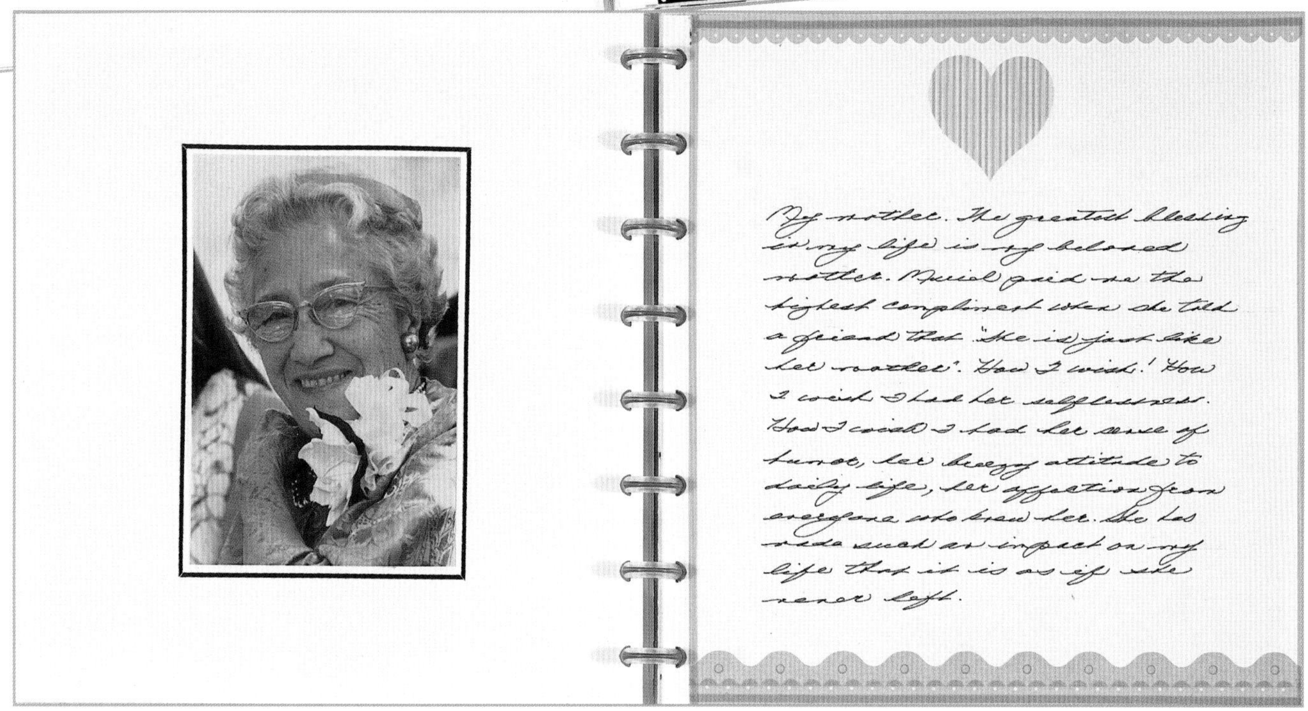
My mother. The greatest blessing
in my life is my beloved
mother. Muriel paid me the
highest compliment when she told
a friend that "She is just like
her mother". How I wish! How
I wish I had her selflessness.
How I wish I had her sense of
humor, her breezy attitude to
daily life, her affection from
everyone who knew her. She has
made such an impact on my
life that it is as if she
never left.

• I decided to use the Rollabind® format to make the book. I cut pages to 8" square and punched them with the Rollabind punch. This system is wonderful because you can add, move, and remove pages with ease. When you have too many pages for the book to close easily, you can simply add bigger rings.

I love my WORK!
Work is a blessing and my work is a great blessing. The Lord has given me a place where I can express the talents He has given me. He has surrounded me with remarkable people, inside and out of the company. I pray that those who come in touch with the company are blessed and encouraged. And see Him.

Work ......

Mrs. Grossman's Thanks-Giving Party Album

Your friends at
Mrs. Grossman's and Paragon Label
invite you to celebrate the blessings of 2002
at our Annual Holiday Party
Saturday, November 23, 2002
3810 Cypress Drive, Petaluma, California
7:00 pm – 11 pm
Please R.S.V.P.
to Ann Corda at 707.763.1700
by November 12, 2002

Because I make almost all of my albums as gifts for family and friends, you can imagine my delight when I received a remarkable album!

Every year, Mrs. Grossman's Thanksgiving holiday party gets better. This is our time to say thank-you to our staff, our reps, customers, and vendors. It is always a perfectly wonderful party and the visionary behind it is none other than our corporate Controller, Michelle Chu, and her assistant Joan Dani.

Last year they transformed our warehouse into a western town in honor of my son's (and my) favorite musical group, the Comstock Cowboys. There were false-front western buildings, a life-sized horse, and activities such as rope twirling during the cocktail hour. When the portals opened for dinner, we were dazzled by the replicas of a period dance hall and saloon.

As you can see in the pictures, the food array was outstanding and the table decorations breathtaking. Everyone was dressed up, many in western attire, and we learned to line dance. What a terrific evening we all had!

In addition to planning and carrying off this grand event, Michelle made one album for Jason and one for me. Talk about a five-star gift! She knows we treasure our memories in photo form. I love being able to share this book with people because through it they can meet so many of the wonderful individuals with whom I am privileged to work.

• In a favorite onyx album, Michelle used a carefully chosen collection of Design Lines and individual theme stickers. She not only captured the feeling and the colors of the event, she told the story of a very special evening.

• Michelle was careful to photograph our guests, our servers, and our staff. She knows that people make the party!

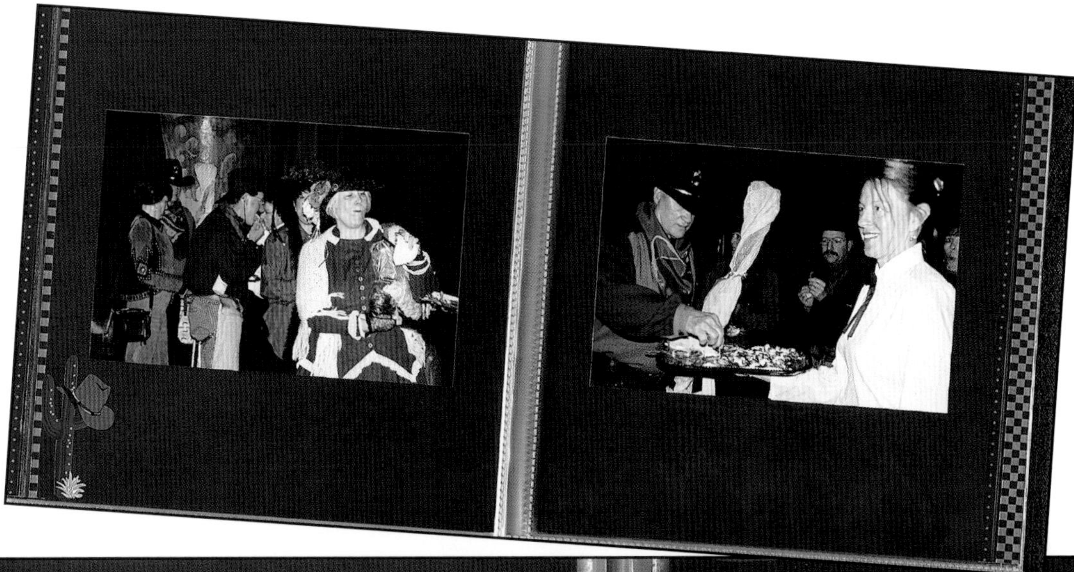

Mrs. Grossman's Paper Company Album

We are just beginning to record the history of Mrs. Grossman's Paper Company in a company scrapbook. We thought this would be a great way to celebrate our 25th anniversary in 2004.

Hunters Point Youth Park

This section is about our very special relationship with the kids of Hunters Point Youth Park, located in one of the most dangerous neighborhoods in San Francisco. A few years ago, we started a program of shipping our "seconds" stickers to Hunters Point. A select group of the young people who spend their after-school hours at the Youth Park have formed a company to package the stickers to be sent off to children's hospitals all across the nation. Child-life specialists use the packets for therapeutic work with their patients and a wonderful relationship has grown between the two groups of children, as thank-you notes pour into Hunters Point. Our friends there have learned how wonderful it is to do things for others. They receive gift certificates for their work, so they enjoy the reward system as well.

our first visit to Hunters Point
Youth Park was exciting!
kids welcomed us, especially Beau

Helping Hands is off to a good start...

many of the kids had never petted a dog before

• This group of pages is all one color to emphasize that they are all one aspect of the company. We chose yellow because these kids bring lots of sunshine into our lives. We cut the right borders down and decorated each with a child so that when they are together as a set, they form a whole group of kids. We used yellow stickers to border all the pages and create continuity. By using yellow and red journaling panels, we could use our favorite hearts for the accents.

we love having the kids at our factory parties

packaging stickers that we donate to children in hospitals

• Because we wanted to get as many photos in as few pages as possible, we pulled the photos together to create blocks—easy on the eye.

Friday the 13th (June 2003) was a lucky day for the Youth Park. Eleven of us joined 50+ others for a major workday.

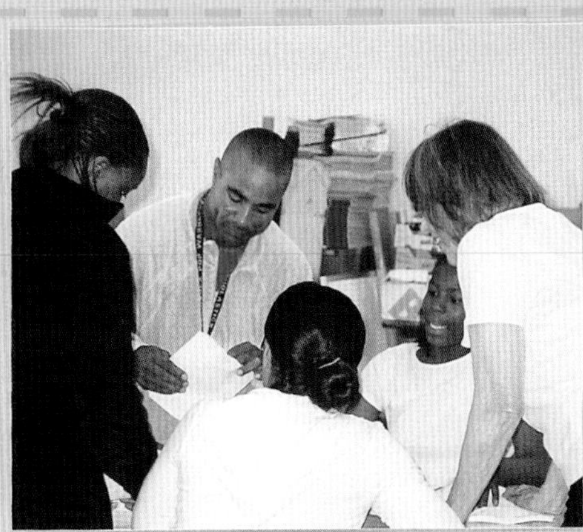

Groundbreaking

In 2000, we broke ground to begin construction on a 50,000 sq.ft. addition to double the size of our corporate headquarters. It was a very exciting day and the official "shovelers" included my son Jason and my brother Bertin. Bertin had designed our first building and was excited to be working on this expansion.

The work progressed beautifully . . . we watched whole walls go up at a time . . . and soon we were walking around, CAREFULLY, within the beginnings of interior walls. One of the exciting things about the new building was that we would have space for a museum, a classroom, and a new retail store, showcasing our products. One day I took a tour of the new store space with my assistant, Alison Hastings, our store manager, Cindy Studdert, and Sue Ferguson, our national class coordinator. It was so exciting.

But the day Jason and I put up the sign and opened the doors to our first tour guests was beyond words. We were mobbed and everyone had a marvelous time. The lines went out the door as our visitors streamed in to see our printing facility, assembly, and packaging departments. We have visitors every day now and we love their enthusiasm for stickers. They even get to take a class and become sticker artists themselves!

Breaking ground
for our addition.
~2000~

CLOCKWISE: *Jason and Andrea ready to greet our tour guests. // Opening Day Tour // A welcoming heart. // Presses ready to roll.*

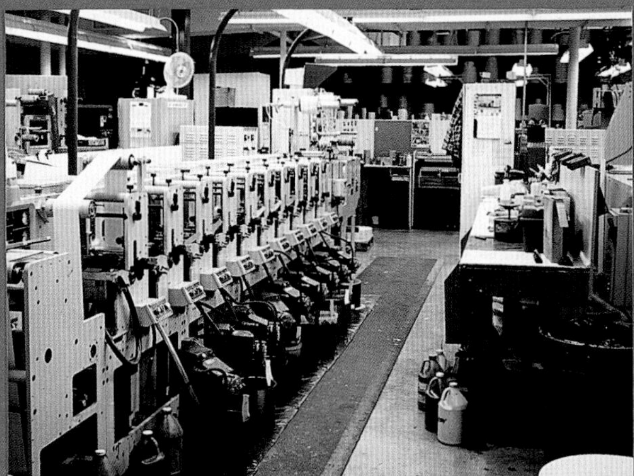

Dog Days of Summer

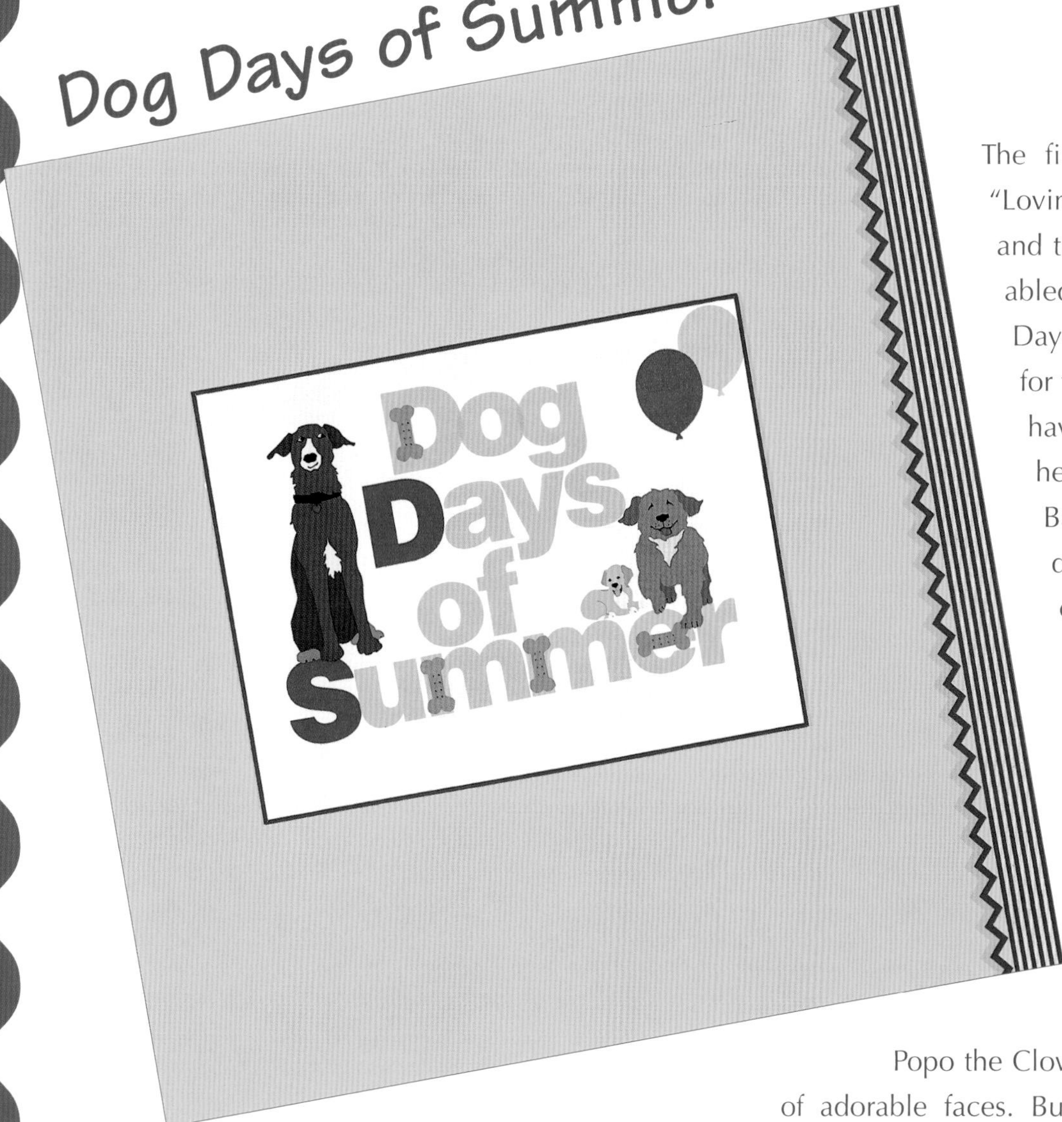

The first year we raised money for "Loving Paws," a local group, raising and training companion dogs for disabled teenagers. Last year our "Dog Days of Summer" party raised funds for three nearby animal shelters. We have so many good friends who help put on the party: Barbara's Bakery®, a neighbor, sends over delicious chips; Clo the Cow comes to dish up yummy Clover® ice cream cones, and Amac® donates lucite boxes for the kids to decorate with stickers. The best fun every year is the hilarity provided by the Shriner clowns. These guys keep us all laughing! They are so amazingly generous with their time. This year, Popo the Clown joined them and painted lots of adorable faces. But the highlight was Kazzy the Camel. This local "pet" is trained as a therapy provider, and she visits nursing homes, hospitals, and senior centers to bring a huge (8 feet tall, 1400 pounds, and growing) surprise and smiles galore to those she meets. She is a special favorite of ours, totally tame and lovable. Who would have thought?

Every year we chose a day to say thank-you to our wonderfully supportive community by inviting them to join us in a day of summertime celebration, to the benefit of various animal groups in our area. Many of us bring our dogs to work, so we are all animal lovers!

In many photos you have one central important image, and several distracting images in the background. With careful cropping, you can create a mosaic focal point that has the energy and feeling of the event. This is also a great way to get several pictures on a page and leave that all-important negative space.

Kazzy the Camel, Shine, Popo and the Shriner clowns helped us raise funds for two animal shelters.

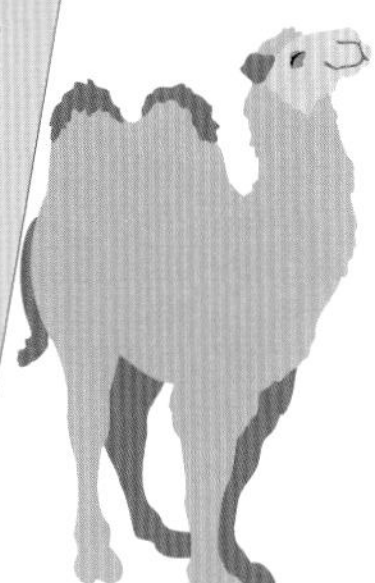

Dogs at Work

By now, nearly everyone knows that at Mrs. Grossman's, our dogs come to work. And their presence is one of the nicest perks of working here! I bring my own five-year-old Australian Shepherd, Beau, and he hangs out under my glass desk in the morning and spends his afternoons napping on his velvet bed behind the chair in my office. But in between, he spends lots of time "managing" the art department, and begging his favorite "aunties" to take him for walks. My son Jason and his wife Kim both work with me, as do their three Aussies and two Toy Pomeranians. One of their Aussies, Angus, is the company mascot and my favorite "Grand-dog." He is the father of Beau and is so clever (I'm not prejudiced) that he knows when it's Monday. He always comes home with me on Mondays for a sleepover!

There are about twelve dogs who are in the office, and several more prefer to use the outdoor runs all day. The MOST fun is when someone gets a new puppy!

The dogs are our best ambassadors of good will. Angus is the narrator and host of the video tape we show our tour guests, so you can imagine how in demand he is to make a personal appearance after each tour. And he performs that job beautifully! All that petting is his pay! Several of the other dogs help him out on particularly busy days. Kids of all ages love our sticker company because they love our dogs and our stickers.

Chip is usually in Jason's arms at all business meetings. Dakota is trained to deliver papers from one department to another. I LOVE to work on the floor—I say it is efficient, but I know it's partly (or mostly) because dogs come for pets the minute I'm at their level.

"Job description:
snuggle, offer
hospitality, guide,
deliver, rest, and
SNUGGLE."

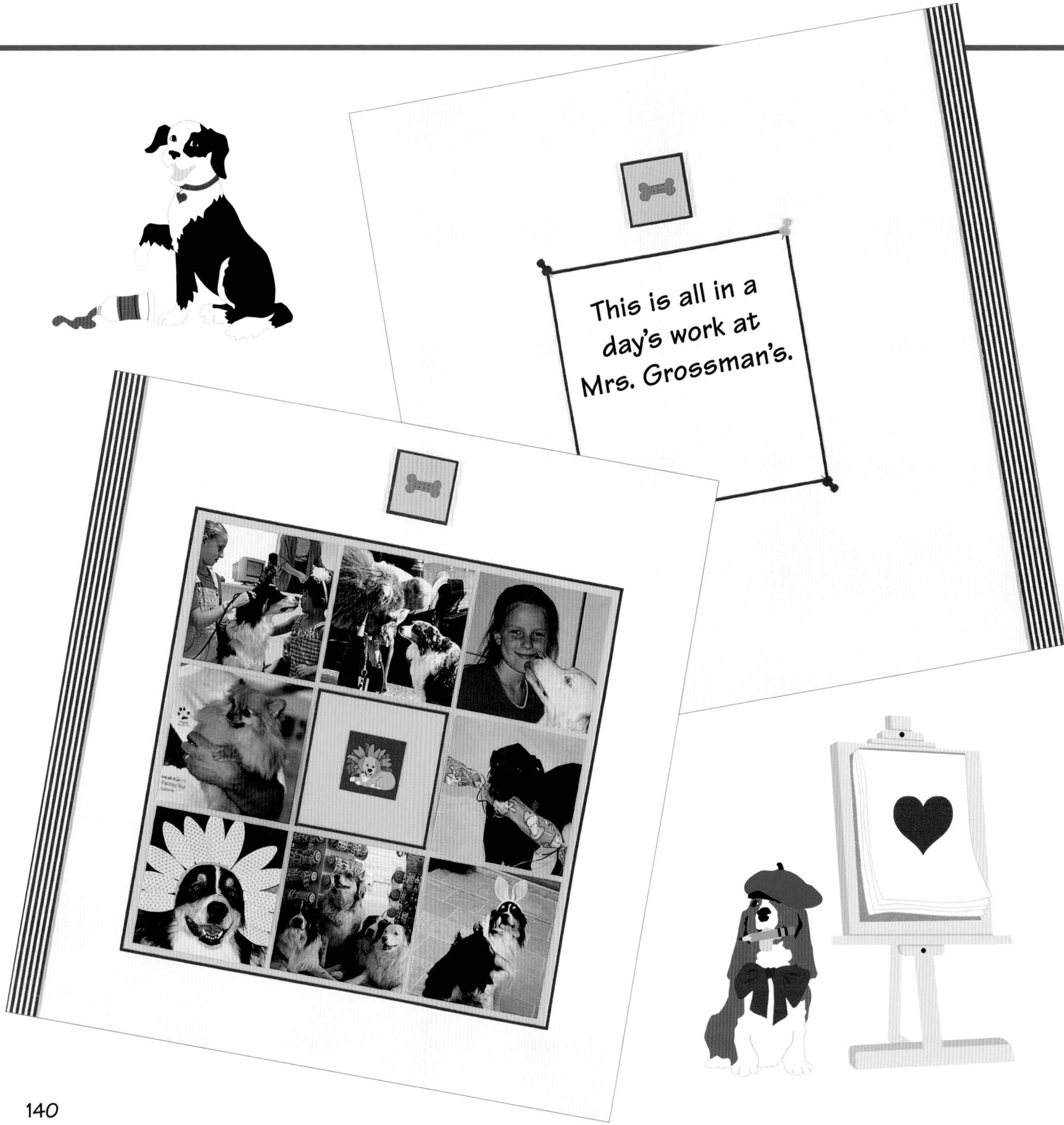
This is all in a
day's work at
Mrs. Grossman's.

Acknowledgments

Andrea Grossman
President

My gratitude goes out to the following people who have played a part in creating this book:

Thank you, Jason, for being such an important part in creating the memories captured here.

Talented people in our art department have given me inspiration and ideas for my album-making, and I thank each one. Some are mentioned in the text, but special thanks to Audrey Giorgi for her contributions to the Baby Boy album.

Thank you Maureen Morrison for the photography seen in "Jason's Wedding Album."

Linda Risbrudt, my dear friend, gives of her time to create and improve some of the albums I make. When we scrapbook together, we both rise to new levels.

Thank you, Shannon McMath Aja, for your help in the digital universe we've been living in during the creation of this book. You are always a step ahead of me. And also thanks to Steve Aja, Shannon's husband, who took all the wonderful photos here at the office and at my home and made those days such fun.

Sherryl Kumli, assistant and cherished friend, dedicated hours each day to make sure the details were taken care of. You'll never hear her say, "That's not my job." Thank you, Sherryl, with all my heart.

Jo Packham, you are an inspiration. Thank you for inviting me to do this book and giving me a peek into your beautiful world.

Sticker Inventory

Used throughout this book:
Stickers:
Artist Gear
Baby Accessories
Baby Things
Baby Toys
Bees
Black-eyed Susan
Camel
Chickadee
Cooking Equipment
Cowboy Boots
Dogs
Dragonflies
Kids
Luggage, etc
Neighborhood Dogs
Palm Tree PW
Penguins
Red Heart
Small Flags
Vellum Grass
Wild West
Woodland Animals
Design Lines:
Basic Red and White
Fourth of July
Children
Rose Petals
Spicy Zig Zags
Water
Vellum Active Edges
Vellum Active Edges, Primary
Vellum Deckle & Lines
Vellum Dots & Stripes
Vellum Dots & Stripes, Primary
Vellum Textile Prints
Vellum Twist & Torn, Primary
Stickers used in featured albums:
Jason's Wedding Album, 36–39:
Henry's Lace Design Lines
Reflections Small Hearts
Rose Petals
Soft Shades Slivers
Wedding Flowers
Fourth of July Albums, 40–45:
Basic Red & White Design Lines
Bunting Design Lines
Flag Stickers
Flag, Small Stickers
Fourth of July Design Lines
Navy & White Basic Design Lines
Reflection Fireworks Sticker
Sliver Design Lines
Vellum Torn-Edge Design Lines, Primary
My Friends Album and Friendship Cards, 46–49:
Flower Stickers
Green Vellum Design Lines
Tahoe Thank-you Album, 50–51:
Sliver Design Lines
Water Design Lines
Virginia City Guest Album, 52–53:
Casual Alphabet
Concerto Design Lines
Cooking and Groceries Stickers
Destinations Texas
Earthtone Design Lines
Great Adventures 1880s Train Sticker
Great Adventures Riverboat
Jean and Bandana Design Lines
Jewel Tone Slivers
Neighborhood Dog Stickers
Spice Design Lines
Western Town Design Lines
Wild West Stickers
Baby Gift Albums, 54–61:
Baby Buggy Stickers
Baby Chick Stickers
Baby Things Stickers
Balloon Stickers, Primary
Cloud Stickers
Easter Baskets Stickers
Julie's Strawberry Stickers-by-the-yard
Kid's Train Sticker
Lace Edging Design Lines
Lamb Sticker
Micro Butterfly Sticker
Pastel Pattern Design Lines
Penguins
Pink Ribbon Vellum Design Lines
Powder Vellum Alphabet
Scalloped Lace Border
Small Reflection Hearts
Swimming Gear
Vellum Active Edges
Vellum Grass Design Line
Vellum Heart Sticker
Vellum Panels
Vellum Polka Dots and Stripes Design Lines
Vellum Rainbow Design Lines
Vellum Squares
Vellum Textile Prints
Bridal Shower Recipe Album, 62–67:
Cooking Equipment
Groceries Stickers
Vellum Design Lines
Israel Album, 70–73:
Opal Seashells Stickers
Columbia River Cruise Album, 74–81:
Blue Casual Alphabet Stickers
Bunting Design Lines
Flag Stickers
Great Adventures Riverboat
Silver Classic Alphabet
Sliver Design Lines
Water Design Lines
Zig Zag Design Lines
Greece Album, 84–91:
Bible Sticker
Cruise Ship Sticker
Greco Columns Design Lines
Water Design Lines
Design Lines
Alaska Album, 92–99:
Celery Vellum Alphabet
Classic Gold Alphabet
Cloud Stickers
Eagle Sticker
Great Adventures Train
Raindrop Stickers
Rainbow Vellum Design Lines
Silverware Stickers
Textile Print Vellum Design Lines
Antarctica Album, 100–111:
Lustre Hearts
Metallic Sliver Design Lines
Penguins Stickers
Reflection Snowflakes
Angola Album and Document Folder, 114–115:
Alphabet Silver PW
Count Your Blessings Album, 116–119:
Alphabet Stickers
Cloud Stickers
Confetti Stickers
Dragonflies Sticker
Jeans & Bandana Design Lines
Neighborhood Dog Stickers
Opalescent Small Flower
Wild Bird Stickers
Wild West Stickers
Thanks-Giving Party Album, 122–127:
Wild West Stickers
Primary Vellum Active Edges Design Lines
Company Album, 128–141:
Artist Gear Stickers
Basic Red & White Design Lines
Home Improvement Design Lines
Kids Stickers
Neighborhood Dog Stickers
Textile Prints Design Lines

The following albums are by Kolo®: Fourth of July Album, Columbia River Cruise Album and Thank-you Album, Alaska Album, and Antarctica Album.

Index